Houses with Stories

A *YANKEE BOOKS* TRAVEL GUIDE

Houses with Stories

From Cottages to Castles,
Landmarks to Literary Sites,
50 Tours of New England's
Most Fascinating Homes

BY MARY MAYNARD

YANKEE BOOKS

Notice: While every care has been taken to ensure the accuracy of the information in this guide, the passage of time will always bring change, and consequently the publisher cannot accept responsibility for errors that may occur.

All prices and opening times quoted here are based on information supplied to us at press time. Dates and rates may change, however, and the prudent traveler will avoid inconvenience by calling ahead.

Book Designer: Sandy Freeman
Cover Designer: Stan Green
About the cover photos: Top: Roseland Cottage, page 67 (R. Perron; f/Stop Pictures). Bottom right: Belcourt Castle, page 18 (C. Smith; f/Stop Pictures). Bottom left: Olson Homestead, page 85 (G. Robinson; f/Stop Pictures).

Library of Congress Cataloging-in-Publication Data

Maynard, Mary
      Houses with stories : from cottages to castles, landmarks to literary sites, 50 tours of New England's most fascinating homes / by Mary Maynard.
         p.   cm. — (Yankee Books Travel Guide)
      Includes index.
      ISBN 0–89909–370–1 paperback
      1. Dwellings—New England—Guidebooks. 2. New England—Tours. I. Title. II. Series.
   F5.M389 1994
   917.404'43—dc20   93-24180
                                                         CIP

Distributed in the book trade by St. Martin's Press

2 4 6 8 10 9 7 5 3 1   paperback

Contents

Introduction

House touring is quickly becoming one of the nation's favorite pastimes. Peeking into the lives of the notorious and famous, the visitor discovers that some of the most fascinating characters were also the quirkiest. And the quirkier the people, the better the story their houses can tell. In New England, every historical home produces a bounty of such stories.

"Home" in New England can mean anything from a house made of paper to a replica of Versailles. The curious, whimsical, magnificent, humble and palatial are all well represented in New England's architectural tales.

Tucked away in the most unlikely places, from Maine to Rhode Island, you'll find homes that range from magnificent mansions filled with priceless treasures to humble hand-hewn cottages dating back to the 1600s. You'll come across dark, brooding structures, behind whose rattling shutters ominous secrets hide, as well as curious and whimsical showpieces, testaments to the incredible Yankee spirit and ingenuity. Some of the oldest houses are steeped in the legend and folklore of witches, pirates, Indians, heroes, villains and, of course, ghosts. They hold a strong fascination for everyone.

While there are well over 600 houses open to the public throughout New England, this book focuses on just a small portion of them. This selection of homes gives you a sampling of some of the most inviting places to visit in New England—and allows you to discover, at your leisure, the intriguing stories of the people who lived here.

You'll read about famous New Englanders—from John F. Kennedy and Mark Twain to Lizzie Borden and Cornelius Vanderbilt. You'll get a preview of the museums that tell stories of the lives of Yankees who forged history, set precedents and examples, and stood up for their rights. From the Revolutionary era to the present day, these tales will entertain you, and explain the history behind New England's *Houses with Stories.*

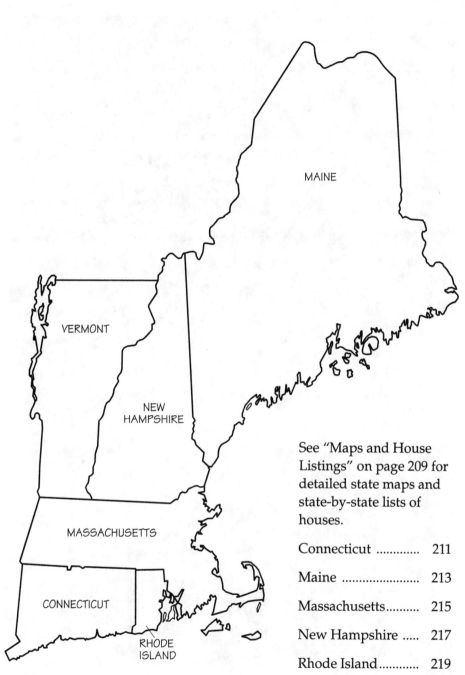

MAINE

VERMONT

NEW
HAMPSHIRE

MASSACHUSETTS

CONNECTICUT

RHODE
ISLAND

See "Maps and House
Listings" on page 209 for
detailed state maps and
state-by-state lists of
houses.

The Great Hall of Belcourt Castle.

Castles in New England

When thinking about the architecture of New England, what usually comes to mind are images of a bucolic countryside dotted with old weathered Colonial saltboxes and quaint little Cape Cod cottages—or a cityscape of impressive Federal bricks and old Victorian brownstones. Except for the remains of a few lavish summer colonies and some stately mansions along the coast, one hardly expects to find anything that compares with the wealth and grandeur of European royalty.

But don't be surprised to see, as you travel the winding country roads of New England, the battlements, turrets and crenellated towers of European-style castles rising high above the treetops. Scattered throughout all six New England states are a number of replicas of medieval Rhineland fortresses, Gothic baronial manors and French chateaux. While some stand mute and deserted, sad witnesses to romantic dreams gone awry, others are still filled with the original priceless treasures and royal trappings of America's first millionaires.

Unlike the castles of foreign lands that were built by the reigning sovereigns as mighty fortresses to guard against invaders, the castles of New England were extravagant imitations built by ordinary men and women as flamboyant testaments to their enormous wealth. Most of these structures were built during the

Gilded Age (1870-98), when great fortunes were to be made and kept in America.

Artisans and workers were brought from all over the world to build these castles. In many cases, whole rooms—complete with tiled floors, hand-carved ceilings, interior wall panels, stained glass windows, priceless tapestries and carpets and massive stone fireplaces with ornate mantels—were imported intact from Europe.

The following is a sampling of that fabulous era of America's Gilded Age when man's—and woman's—home was truly a castle.

Abbadia Mare

Hammond Castle Museum
Gloucester, Massachusetts
1929

80 Hesperus Avenue
Gloucester, Mass.
508-283-2080

OPEN:
Mid-May–
December
Daily: 10–4
January–mid-May
Thur–Sat: 10–4
Sun: 1–4

ADMISSION:
Inquire for prices.

Abbadia Mare (Abbey by the Sea), better known as Hammond Castle, rises up from the rocky shores of Cape Ann, towering over the Reef of Norman's Woe, the poetic setting for Longfellow's "Wreck of the Hesperus." It was built by John Hayes Hammond, Jr., a colorful and ingenious inventor. Hammond wanted his castle to serve not only as his home but also as a place to house his vast collection of antique and medieval art objects.

Hammond, the son of wealthy parents, had summered in Gloucester most of his life. As a result of a visit to the laboratory of Thomas A. Edison in his young teens, John developed a desire to become an inventor. His early experiments with electricity and radio waves resulted in hundreds of patents in the field of radio electronics. One of his first experiments involved using radio waves to control an unmanned boat. HIs tests and this invention threw the local fishermen into a panic as they spotted this "ghost ship" silently maneuvering through the rocky waters off the Gloucester coast.

Hammond began collecting art during his travels to Europe in 1924, having been deeply influenced by his friend, art collector Isabella Stewart Gardner (see page 82). In 1926, he married, then purchased the property just a mile down the coastline from his parents' home. In planning his home he ensured that it would accommodate his numerous treasures. In fact, during the construction, he made several additional trips to Europe, each time buying pieces to add to his large collection. "As I collected my pieces," he wrote in 1929, "I had the house changed foot by foot to house my collection. I cabled 83 changes from Italy; one wing was changed to fit a bed."

The focal point of the castle, and what determined its design the most, was an enormous pipe organ that Hammond designed and had built. It spans eight stories of the castle; an 85-foot tower was constructed to house it. Many famous musicians contributed their ideas and help with the organ and grand concerts are still given here periodically throughout the year.

The Great Hall, which was designed to house the organ, includes an enormous fifteenth-century fireplace. On the opposite wall from the fireplace is a small chapel where Hammond liked to serve his guests their pre-dinner cocktails. Next to the chapel is the Bishop's Chair Alcove, a favorite spot of Hammond's. He often propped himself up here with pil-

Hammond Castle displays many fine examples of European art.

lows late at night and, by the light of a hand-held flashlight, read a book before retiring. Later, when the house was opened to visitors, he would often hide behind a screen in the alcove to watch "the curious."

Beyond the Great Hall is the sunny, glass-roofed courtyard where imported fifteenth-century French house facades surround a heated swimming pool. Hammond ingeniously wired the ceiling so that he could create any kind of weather for his guests that they wished—from soft gray mist to a loud clapping thunder shower; from sunlit days to moonlit nights.

Visitors who tour the castle will see and hear many little anecdotes relating to Hammond's unusual sense of humor and his love of the macabre. One classic enxample of this involves a fifteenth-century painting

The House of Surprises on Eastern Point

On the opposite side of Gloucester Harbor, almost directly across from Hammond Castle, sits another medieval structure with towers, archways and latticed windows. Beauport, the former home of Henry Davis Sleeper, a leading interior designer of the 1920s, dominates Eastern Point, acting as a landmark for boats entering the harbor. Eclectic is the word most often used to describe this castle.

Although smaller than Hammond Castle and less imposing from the outside, it is the contents of the house that draw thousands of visitors here each year. Sleeper was an avid collector of antiques and built his house around his collections. He began his house in 1907 with three rooms and continued adding to it until the time of his death in 1934. By then Beauport contained over 40 rooms.

Sleeper planned each room around a theme, as he put it, "to recapture some of the spirit of a specific mood or phase or period of our American life from the time of Plymouth down through the Revolution and the early republic." Achieving this aim, the house is a series of strange and unexpected angles, nooks and crannies and surprising spaces, all filled with priceless antiques. Sleeper's use of light to create dramatic effects is particularly appealing throughout the house. It has been called "the most fascinating house in America." For information call 508-283-0800.

of the Martydom of Saint Romanus of Antioch that hangs in the dining room. When entertaining dinner guests Hammond would relate the story of how the saint had his tongue pulled out by its roots. He would then signal the servants to bring in the entrée. With great flair he would uncover a large silver platter, revealing a freshly cooked cow's tongue!

Another example of his passion for playing tricks on his guests is his arrangement of one of the guest bedrooms, the Purple Room. He habitually reserved this room for a guest who was inclined to drink too much before retiring. All the doors in the room were wallpapered to exactly match the walls. When the guest awoke in the morning, he would be completely disoriented. Much to the amusement of those waiting in the breakfast room below, the sleepy, befuddled guest would have to ring for a servant to help him find his way out.

There are many more rooms to explore at Hammond Castle, priceless objects to see, three floors of galleries housed in the tower and a gift shop. The castle is surrounded by woodland paths for walking and scenic spots for picnics. The Hammond Castle is owned by the Hammond Castle Museum, Inc., a nonprofit corporation dedicated to stimulating interest in the museum as a focal point for the arts and as a performing arts center. Throughout the year there are many events, such as concerts, costume balls and film festivals. If you so choose, you can even rent the castle for your own event.

Napoleon's Retreat

Castle in the Clouds
Moultonborough, New Hampshire
1913

Moultonborough,
N.H.
603-476-2512

OPEN:
May–mid-June
Weekends: 10–5

Mid-June–
mid-October
Daily: 9–5
Weekends: 10–4

ADMISSION:
Inquire for prices.

The red-roofed peaks and gables of this lavish home poke out through the lush green treetops high up on the western slopes of the Ossipee Mountains in Moultonborough, New Hampshire. Seen from many points far below, where the large and beautiful Lake Winnipesaukee spreads for miles, it's understandable why it has been dubbed Castle in the Clouds by all who visit.

This is the story of the man who built this scenic wonder. It took thousands of workmen, millions of dollars and many years to build, and its tale rivals the best of the Horatio Alger stories.

Thomas Gustave Plant was a poor boy, one of several children. At the age of 13, he left his hometown of Bath, Maine, to seek his fortune in Boston, where he found employment in a shoe factory. Although small in stature, he emulated his hero, Napoleon. With his inventive mind and forceful personality, he quickly worked his way up to a leading position. His many inventions, which he was clever enough to patent, soon paid him so royally that he was actually able to buy the shoe factory—and several others as well.

He retired while still in his 50s, with an estimated wealth of over $21 million. He then proceeded to build his dream castle. He purchased, with some bullying, the entire side of Ossipee Mountain, from its peak down to the lake. This encompassed a total of 6,300 acres, with a view extending as far as the eye could see (75 miles on a clear day).

In 1913, he began construction on his home. His inventive mind is evidenced by the modern innovations he included—a central vacuum cleaning system, an intercom system, skylights, forced-hot-air

The stone walls of Castle in the Clouds were fashioned by hand from local granite.

heating, a self-cleaning oven, fancy shower stalls and a fire detection system. He even had his own fire engine on the property.

The house, which he named Lucknow after Napoleon's retreat, is made almost entirely of stone—granite blasted out of the surrounding hillside. Plant's design called for each stone to be shaped in a pentagon, and the mortar recessed so that it appeared as though no mortar had been used at all. (It was said that it took one mason a whole day to cut and lay three stones.) The roof was made from Spanish slate, all exterior and interior woodwork was hand-hewn, and many of the brass and leaded glass windows were hand-painted with scenes from the estate.

Plant was considered to be an eccentric, and any number of strange tales have been told about him. While building his house, for instance, he fell madly in love with his young secretary, Olive Dewey (26 years younger and 12 inches taller than Plant). One morning, his wife came down to breakfast and found a check for $1 million rolled up in her table napkin. She took the hint and left the same day. Shortly after, Plant married young Olive.

The Plants did not like to entertain large groups in their home. There were only two guest bedrooms in the house and the dining room table sat no more than a dozen people. Instead, Plant built an exclusive country club on his property (Bald Peak Colony Club, which is still in operation today—and still exclusive). He opened the membership to his friends, who stayed in private cottages or dormitories surrounding the club. Membership was highly expensive ($2,500 at that time) and extremely selective—no one was allowed to drink, swear or weigh over 200 pounds!

Mirror Images

Thomas Plant, the builder of Castle in the Clouds, had many imitators and colleagues with similar tastes and visions. One such builder was Herbert Dumaresq. He also chose the Lakes Region of New Hampshire to build his dream house, Kona Farm, in Moultonborough. Although Dumaresq was not from a poor family, as Plant was, he was orphaned at the age of 10 when his parents died in drowning accidents.

In 1867, at the age of 16, Herbert went to work for the fledgling department store Jordan Marsh in Boston. Like Plant, he, too, worked his way to the top. By the time he retired in 1900 he had become a full partner—having married and divorced the boss's daughter. (Divorce was considered so scandalous at that time that all references to Herbert were deleted from the store's centennial history.)

Dumaresq moved to Moultonborough after discovering the perfect spot to build his dream house, which he named Kona Farm. Perched on a hilltop overlooking Lake Winnipesaukee, the large, impressive mansion with its red tile roof and native stones bears a striking resemblance to Castle in the Clouds.

Although Dumaresq and his second wife spent many happy years at Kona Farm, he met with much the same financial fate as Plant. He invested unwisely, suffering great financial losses, and eventually lost his home to creditors.

Today, Kona Farm is operated as a guest house and restaurant and it is open to the public for breakfast and dinner. For information and reservations call 603-253-4900.

Throughout his life, Plant was known as a generous employer and contributed much to charity. One of his gifts was the Plant Memorial Home, built in 1917 in his hometown of Bath, in memory of his mother. It was a retirement home for senior citizens with small pensions. Ironically, Plant himself was to end up destitute, having made many bad investments and losing heavily in the stock market crash. In the late 1930s, he was forced into bankruptcy. The bank took over possession of Lucknow, but he and his wife were allowed to live there until his death in 1941.

The property was bought in 1956 by Richard Robie, another self-made millionaire, who rose from a 15-year-old bank messenger to become the president of the International Avis Rent-A-Car System. Robie restored Lucknow, changing the name to Castle in the Clouds, and opened it to the public.

Castle in the Clouds is now owned by Castle Springs Company, a bottling facility that takes advantage of the natural spring water that is available on the property. The house and grounds are still open to the public, and visitors are taken on a guided tour of both the castle and the bottling plant. Along the winding, hilly entrance road to the castle, there are several well-marked natural wonders to enjoy. The Fall of Song and Bridal Veil are 50-foot waterfalls that plummet into a rocky ravine; Little Pebble is an oddly shaped 300-ton boulder. There are 85 miles of carriage roads for hiking and horseback riding (stables are on the premises), and a nice picnic area beside Shannon Pond just below the castle.

Gillette Castle

Hadlyme, Connecticut
1929

67 River Road
Hadlyme, Conn.
203-526-2336

OPEN:
Late April–
mid-October
Daily: 10–5

ADMISSION:
Inquire for prices.

William Gillette had every intention of building his castle on the outer edges of the northern peninsula of Long Island. He had, in fact, already ordered vast amounts of building supplies to be sent to Greenport, the location where he planned to start construction. But while on a cruise up the Connecticut River, he was struck by the beauty of a lofty, tree-lined ridge rising high above the river on the east bank, close to the Chester-Hadlyme ferry station. It was the highest peak in a series of seven hills along this part of the river, known locally as The Seven Sisters.

Not one to procrastinate, Gillette immediately set about purchasing the ridge and the surrounding acreage (122 acres with a shorefront of almost ¾ mile). He arranged for the heavy steel and iron materials he had already purchased to be sent up on barges from Long Island.

The year was 1913, and William Gillette was at the peak of his acting career. He was considered at that time one of the great figures of the American stage, having brought to life the legendary detective Sherlock Holmes. So impressive was his portrayal of the fictitious super sleuth that for generations theatergoers had nourished the belief that Holmes was, indeed, a real person.

Gillette literally carved his castle out of the rock formation of the hillside, keeping 22 skilled masons at work for almost five years. Near the ferry he built a tramway to carry workmen and materials up to the worksite. He drafted his own architectural drawings and planned every detail. He patterned the castle after a Rhenish fortress, and built it entirely of native granite. He named his castle the Seventh Sister, after the hill it graces.

The interior of the castle is filled with Gillette's ingenuity. Providing entrance to the 24 rooms of the castle are a total of 47 doors, all of them hand-carved from southern white oak. Each is worked by a unique, intricate system of wooden locks and bolts of Gillette's own design. His other whimsical inventions include a hidden bar that only Gillette knew the trick to revealing, furniture that slides to and fro on metal tracks, and strategically placed mirrors (so that Gillette could observe his guests undetected).

The castle remains today much as Gillette left it when he died in 1937. The enormous living room, 50 feet by 30 feet, is dominated by a floor-to-ceiling fieldstone fireplace, and encircled overhead by wooden balconies. Woven straw mats set into the hand-carved wall paneling add an unusual decorating touch, while bright floral overstuffed chairs and divans give the massive room an almost homey feeling. The conservatory just off the living room is filled with plants and a miniature waterfall.

His private study, bedroom, library and art gallery are still filled with most of the original furnishings

Gillette Castle was originally planned to be built on Long Island.

and many of his personal mementos. Gillette was very fond of cats, and kept up to 17 in the house when he lived there. Throughout the castle, many objects made of ceramic, stone and wood are in the shape of cats.

The outdoor terraces and windows offer spectacular views of the Connecticut River. There are plenty of paths and hiking trails to explore, and stone gazebos for picnicking. The castle is operated by the Connecticut State Park and Forest Commission.

The nearby Chester-Hadlyme ferry, the second oldest ferry in continuous use in Connecticut, provides a pleasant 10-minute ride across the Connecticut River from Memorial Day through Columbus Day and on weekends until Christmas. Visitors can catch the ferry in Chester on Route 148, at the ferry depot.

Entertainment on a Grand Scale

Along the banks of the Connecticut River, just a few miles upstream from Gilette Castle in nearby East Haddam, is a large Victorian structure known far and wide as the Goodspeed Opera House. It was built in 1876 for William H. Goodspeed, who had a large and prosperous shipyard in town and built steamboats that once cruised the Connecticut River.

The Opera House offered the best in entertainment and became a popular tourist destination during its heyday. Goodspeed spared no expense in the decoration of this elaborate showplace—he built it six stories high, reserving the upper floors for the theater and balcony.

With the decline in steamboat travel, the Opera House fell into neglect and disrepair. In 1963 an enterprising group refurbished it—using much of the original furnishings—and established it as a premiere summer musical theatre. While many of the shows presented here are musical revivals, several have gone on to become Broadway hits, including "Annie," "Man of La Mancha" and "Shenandoah."

Three productions are presented each season. For reservations call 203-873-8668.

The Royal Stables

Bellevue Avenue
Newport, R.I.
401-846-0669

OPEN:
February–
Memorial Day
Daily: 10–4

Memorial Day–
Mid-October
Daily: 9–5

Mid-October–
November
Daily: 10–4

December 1–
January 3
Mon–Sat: 10–3
Sun: 10–1.
Concerts & tea at 2

ADMISSION:
Inquire for prices.

Belcourt Castle

Newport, Rhode Island
1891

Belcourt Castle was designed and built at the height of the Gilded Age when Newport, Rhode Island, was the favorite summer resort of America's newly made millionaires. From 1890 to 1914, a time when great fortunes were to be made in this country, such local royalty as the Vanderbilts and the Astors built their summer "cottages" (castles, actually) in this small city by the bay. Many of their homes not only copied European palaces, but were filled with priceless treasures imported from all over the world.

Belcourt, a 60-room castle patterned after a Louis XIII hunting lodge at Versailles, was built for Oliver Hazard Perry Belmont, son of August Belmont (who built Belmont Park Race Track in New York). Oliver inherited his father's love of horses and had his castle designed not only for himself but for his horses as well. Specially designed massive front doors were large enough for both horses and carriages to enter the front hall. (It is said that if you turn the carpet back in the front hallway, you can still see the hoof prints.)

Definitely a bachelor's pad (even to the floral bachelor's-buttons incorporated in the design of damask wall coverings) the castle had only one big bedroom and few baths. But no expense was spared in other quarters. Belmont imported European craftsmen to create intricate carvings and detailed ceilings, and installed solid gold and sterling silver door hinges and knobs. The main dining room is a copy of the mirror room at Versailles. The French Gothic Ballroom, 70 feet long, has the largest collection of medieval stained glass in America. The castle was furnished with rare antiques acquired from four continents.

At the time the castle was built, and in spite of all this splendor, it was the south wing—the stables—that drew most of the attention. In a small city with a penchant for the outrageous, Belmont's stables, said to be the finest in America, were the talk of the town. The walls were tiled in white and bordered in maroon and scarlet—the Belmont colors. The stalls were upholstered and paneled as luxuriously as the castle itself. Box stalls for special horses were at each end, with 26 standing stalls in between. Each of the 30 horses kept here wore a white linen blanket embroidered in gold with the Belmont coat-of-arms. They had equipment changes for morning, afternoon and evening. Their harness fittings were of sterling silver. It was said that the handmade English brick floor behind the stalls was covered in sand, and that 160-foot-long paintings were drawn into the sand daily.

Two years after Oliver built his bachelor's dream castle, he married the leading socialite of Newport, newly divorced Alva Vanderbilt. Their home soon became the scene of some of Newport's most spectacu-

This "summer cottage" was home to the Belmont family—and their horses.

lar parties, often the setting for some outrageous happenings.

Belcourt has often been credited with popularizing the automobile in America. Newport's first automobile festival was held at Belcourt in 1899. Socialites, delighting in this newfangled machine, competed in obstacle races on the broad lawns by dodging

Tennis, Anyone?

The approximate four-mile stretch of Bellevue Avenue from Memorial Boulevard in downtown Newport to the beginning of Ocean Drive is lined with several other mansions that are open to the public. Many of them are maintained by the Preservation Society of Newport. The Newport Casino was built in 1880 when lawn games—tennis, bowling and croquet—were the rage. Located at the opposite end of Bellevue Avenue from Belcourt Castle, the casino was considered the most complete resort facility in the country. Originally an elaborate men's club, the building encircled a large courtyard adorned with fountains and flowers. It housed a café, theater and bachelor apartments. Men's championship tennis tournaments were held here from 1881 to 1914, with the best seats in the spectator section reserved for the Vanderbilts, Astors and Belmonts.

Many changes have taken place over the years to this rambling, shingled landmark building designed by Stanford White. The courtyard and its immaculately groomed tennis courts remain, but now ladies as well as gents are allowed to play here. The Virginia Slims Hall of Fame Invitational championship tournament is held here annually. No longer an exclusive playground for the very rich, the 12 grass courts are now open to the public.

The Tennis Hall of Fame and the world's largest Tennis Museum, established in 1954, now occupy two floors. Together, they encompass a huge collection of tennis memorabilia, trophies, photographs and exhibits from around the world. Call 401-849-3990 for more information.

The La Forge Casino Restaurant on the ground floor is open daily for meals. Ask to be seated on The Porch, where you can usually watch a game in progress (particularly at Sunday brunch). For reservations, call 401-847-0418.

dummy figures of animals, pedestrians and policemen. The cars, thought of as toys at that time, were decorated with garlands of flowers and streamers, and were used mainly for joyriding up and down fashionable Bellevue Avenue.

Belcourt, like Newport itself, has weathered many changes since then. While most of the grand mansions of the Gilded Age have become the property of preservation societies and associations, Belcourt is the only one that is still privately owned and lived in. Since 1957, the castle and grounds have been owned by the Harold B. Tinney family. It is filled with their personal collection of priceless art treasures and antiques, and is open to the public.

The Great Hall of the Breakers, home to three generations of the Vanderbilt family.

Magnificent Mansions

The mansions of New England are huge, rambling, ostentatious homes that were built between 1870 and 1898. They are representative of the enormous wealth of the time, and were constructed so that their owners could host lavish parties and entertain on a grand scale.

The houses sometimes contained as many as 100 rooms and were often copies of French or Roman villas or English country estates. They required almost limitless funds for upkeep, and huge staffs to run them. When the maintenance finally became prohibitive—after income tax laws came into effect and servants turned to factories and mills for better wages—many of them were turned into inns or schools; some were destroyed by fire. A few, however, have survived intact and are kept as house museums.

The following are a few outstanding examples of homes that certainly deserve the moniker of "magnificent," as well as some glimpses into the lives of the people who built them.

A Newport Cottage

Ochre Point Avenue
Newport, R.I.
401-847-6543

OPEN:
April 4–
September 30
Daily: 10–5

July 4–Labor Day
Daily: 10–5
Sat: 10–6

October 1–
November 1
Daily: 10–5

November 29–
December 30
Daily: 3–7
Sat–Sun: 11–7

Closed December
24 and 25

ADMISSION:
Inquire for prices.

The Breakers

Newport, Rhode Island
1895

When Cornelius Vanderbilt II's brick-and-frame Newport mansion, The Breakers, burned to the ground in 1892, he immediately began construction on a replacement home. This one, built on the foundation of the first, was to be completely fireproof. The location of the Breakers on Ochre Point (so named for the distinctive color of the cliffs in front of the house) is still considered one of the most beautiful sites on the northeast Atlantic coast.

Vanderbilt selected renowned architect Richard Morris Hunt to design the new Breakers. Hunt had already designed several Newport mansions, including the elaborate Marble House for William K. Vanderbilt (Cornelius II's brother) and Ochre Court for Ogden Goelet. Hunt gladly accepted this new challenge. He was determined to build the Vanderbilts a mansion that would surpass the magnificence and grandeur of his previous works. He modeled the new Breakers after Italian Renaissance villas of Genoa and Turin. Hunt quickly became known as the man who "found Newport a town of wood and left it a town of marble."

The mansion's support structure contains no wood, but consists of a great latticework of steel beams that support the masonry and exterior limestone blocks. Even today, with the technical advancement in materials and design, engineers agree that its ingenious fireproof construction could not be improved upon. To further remove the hazard of fire, an enormous heating plant was built beneath the caretaker's lodge. It was joined to the basement of the house by a wide tunnel (said to be wide enough to drive a team of horses through) and barred at each end with steel doors. Several hundred tons of coal could be safely

stored in the underground boiler room.

To complete the four-story mansion of 70 rooms (33 of which were for servants, on the top floor) and 30 baths, Hunt imported marble and alabaster from Italy and Africa, Caen stone from France and rare woods and mosaics from five continents. Artisans and craftsmen, also imported from Europe, worked at a feverish pitch to complete the mansion in two years.

The Breakers is considered the most magnificent of all the Newport mansions. The Great Hall rises over 45 feet through two full floors. The second floor is enclosed by an intricately scrolled wrought-iron balcony with bronze railing. The Grand Salon was completely assembled in France, down to the last detail of painting and gilding, by expert French cabinetmakers. It was then disassembled, crated and shipped to Newport. To ensure perfection, the same French craftsmen were sent along with it to reassemble the room in The Breakers. As to furnishings, Cornelius Vanderbilt IV was to write, "Tons of crated treasures from Italy and France arrived weekly and were dragged in great wagons to The Breakers' site. To erect this great villa (which they intended to oc-

The Breakers is considered the most magnificent mansion in Newport.

cupy only ten weeks of the year) my grandparents spent $5 million."

The Breakers was completed just in time for the debut of the Vanderbilts' oldest daughter, Gertrude. It was an elaborate party, with footmen dressed in the maroon livery of the Vanderbilt family stationed on each step of the marble stairway in the Great Hall. Gold cigarette cases and fans were given out as favors to the 300 guests who arrived at midnight for an

---

Horse Sense

A visit to the Breakers Stables, preserved much as it looked during the height of the Gilded Age, gives a special insight into the splendor of Newport society at that time.

The handsomely restored brick building (it suffered a serious fire in the 1960s) was built a mile away from the mansion in 1895 by Cornelius Vanderbilt. The Vanderbilts, as well as some of their neighbors, preferred to build their stables away from their beautiful homes for aesthetic reasons. A direct telephone line to the house brought a horse and carriage to the front door of the mansion within minutes.

A large carriage room dominates the ground floor of the stables, which is filled with more than two dozen vintage vehicles, among them Alfred Vanderbilt's famous "Venture." Twenty-six stalls and two box stalls, all in pristine condition, stand empty—but other rooms are brought to life by a fine collection of photographs and mementos of the "coaching parade," a daily event. Cleveland Amory, in his classic book on the subject of Newport society, *The Last Resorts*, described the coaching parade as "a spectacle never equaled at any other resort."

The parade took place on Bellevue Avenue every weekday at 3 P.M. Members of Newport's high society, dressed in their finery, paraded up and down the avenue in their elegant horse-drawn coaches. "Everything was spick and span," writes Amory. "The horses were groomed and currycombed within an inch of their lives," and the drivers, in shiny black boots, dazzling white pants, and shiny gold buttons on their uniforms, "looked as if they had emerged not from stables at all, but from ladies' boudoirs."

For hours and information call 401-847-1000.

---

elaborate supper and spectacular ball. (Gertrude later married Harry Payne Whitney and established the Whitney Museum of American Art.)

For all their wealth, however, the Vanderbilts' lives were marked by tragedy. Of the seven children of Cornelius II and Alice, four died tragically. Daughter Alice died from a childhood illness at age five; son William, trained to be the head of the "House of Vanderbilt," died of typhoid while a junior at Yale; son Alfred died on the *Lusitania* when it was sunk in World War I; and son Reginald died of chronic alcoholism. The only living son, Cornelius III, was disinherited by his father and never forgiven for marrying what the older Vanderbilt considered "a frivolous woman."

Only a year after The Breakers was completed, Cornelius II suffered a severe stroke and died in 1899 at the age of 56, barely having had a chance to enjoy his new mansion. Alice continued to live another 40 years, summering at The Breakers until the end of her life. The house, with all its original furnishings, was inherited by the youngest child, Gladys, who married a Hungarian nobleman and became the Countess Laszlo Szechenyi. Following her husband's death she maintained the mansion, renting it to the Preservation Society of Newport County for $1 a year, and keeping an apartment on the upper floor for herself. Following her death, it was purchased in its entirety by the Society, which maintains it today.

The House that Rode on a Train

120 Sever Street
Brookline, Mass.
617-277-8943

OPEN:
March–January
Tues–Sat: 10–4:15
Sun: 1–4:15

ADMISSION:
Inquire for prices.

Longyear Historical Society and Museum
Brookline, Massachusetts
1 8 9 0

John Munro Longyear was a noted mining engineer who uncovered the great mineral deposits of the North Lake region of the United States and the rich coal deposits of Spitzbergen, Norway. He built himself a magnificent 66-room mansion on a cliff in Marquette, Michigan, overlooking the waters of Lake Superior. Here he, his wife and five children lived happily from 1892 until 1902.

In 1902, a railroad line was built at the foot of his property, ruining his view of the lake and spoiling the tranquility of the area. Fortunately, having made a fortune in his successful business transactions, he was independently wealthy. He could afford to move his house anywhere he wanted to.

Moving a 66-room stone-and-brick mansion under any circumstances would pose problems. To make matters more complex, Longyear decided to move his family to Boston, Massachusetts—some 1,300 miles away by rail. After looking around for the perfect spot, he decided to reconstruct his home once again, on the top of a hill—Fisher Hill in Brookline, Massachusetts.

The house was dismantled piece by piece. Each block of stone was carefully numbered, wrapped in straw and cloth and loaded aboard a train. It took 190 railroad cars to carry it all from northern Michigan to Brookline. When it arrived, hundreds of horses and wagons were needed to haul the material from the train station in Boston out to Brookline, then up the high hill to the site where the house was to be rebuilt.

Surprisingly, there was very little damage during shipping—most windows, doors and other structural units were reused without change. During construction, however, it was decided to add a wing to the original house, and the mansion was increased to 100 rooms—including a bowling alley in the basement. All in all, the project took three years to complete.

The Longyears were devoted to many philanthropic endeavors and cultural causes during their years in Brookline. One such project was the development of a printing press and related techniques to substantially extend the use of the Braille system. One of their most significant accomplishments, however, was preserving and maintaining the effects of Mary Baker Eddy, founder of the Christian Science religion and the *Christian Science Monitor*.

After her husband's death in 1922, Mrs. Longyear, a devout worker in Christian Science, spent her remaining years collecting, establishing and maintaining these effects under the auspices of the Longyear Foundation, which she founded. She eventually purchased five other houses in New England where Mary Baker Eddy had lived and/or worked. Today these houses are maintained by the Longyear Foundation and are open to the public.

This massive stone and brick structure was moved 1,300 miles from Michigan to Massachusetts.

"The house that rode on a train" is now a museum, owned and operated by the Longyear Historical Society. The museum galleries exhibit historic records, photographs, portraits and artifacts depicting the history and significance of the life and achievements of Mary Baker Eddy and the early pioneer workers associated with her.

Mary's Legacy

The Longyear Historical Society maintains a series of homes and historical sites throughout Massachusetts and New Hampshire that chronicle the life of Mary Baker Eddy, the founder of Christian Science.

In Swampscott, Massachusetts, at 23 Paradise Road (617-599-1853) is the house where Eddy was living in 1866 when she slipped on the ice and was severely injured. Presented in this historic house is the account of her accident, her recovery and the revelation that led to her discovery of Christian Science.

A year later she moved to the Squire Bagley House in Amesbury at 277 Main Street (617-388-1361), where she began her first teaching manual, *The Science of Man.* This house is appointed with many of the original furnishings. The following year she completed her manuscript at the home of Alanson Wentworths, 133 Central Street, in Stoughton, Massachusetts (617-344-3904). All of these houses, including two others in New Hampshire, are open to the public—some year-round and others from May to October. For more information call 617-277-8943.

In Boston, The Christian Science Center, a complex of modern buildings dominated by a large fountain and reflecting pool, offers daily tours. A unique experience of sight and sound is a walk through the Mapparium, a 30-foot-wide stained-glass globe with a footbridge through its center. Visitors are encouraged to test their echo as they walk through. Call 617-450-2000 for more information.

America Wants a Better Bathroom

The Great House
Ipswich, Massachusetts
1927

Argilla Road
Ipswich, Mass.
617-356-4070

OPEN:
On special occasions
and for group tours.

ADMISSION:
Inquire for prices.

Prior to the 1920s, the bathroom was an unmentionable subject for most American homeowners. The transition from the outhouse to indoor plumbing—for those who could afford it—was considered a major cultural advancement. Still, most of these new facilities were located in the corner of a dark basement, or in very utilitarian rooms with Spartan furnishings.

Then along came Richard Teller Crane, Jr. Crane was the son and heir of the founder of the Crane Company, one of the leading American industrial corporations in the early development of such things as steam power, electrical generation, heating and ventilation, refrigeration, railroad transportation, elevators and piping.

When Crane took over his father's company in 1914, he concentrated his efforts on the manufacturing of plumbing valves and fittings, making the Crane Company the largest manufacturer of plumbing supplies in the world. By 1924, determined to upgrade the lavatory and to "make America want a better bathroom," he launched one of the most extensive advertising campaigns in the country, allocating $1 million for his project. He hired designers to create the first practical, decorative bathroom ensembles, and he took his show on the road. Housing this new luxurious bathroom ensemble in a fleet of specially designed buses, his troop of salespeople traveled all over America, showing off the latest status symbol for homeowners.

His elegant bathroom created a sensation wherever it traveled, and every homeowner wanted one. The demand for his fixtures reached far and wide. King Hussein of Hedjaz had one installed in the royal palace at Mecca, and when Frank Lloyd Wright designed the Imperial Hotel in Tokyo, each suite was equipped with the latest in Crane plumbing fixtures.

Nothing did more to advance the status of the bathroom than the lavish movie productions of Hollywood giants, such as Cecil B. DeMille. When Gloria Swanson, one of the most glamorous stars of the 1920s, was seductively filmed by DeMille amid foaming bubbles in a dramatic marble tub, the distinction of the bathroom was ensured.

Crane's summer home, The Great House, was built in 1925 on Castle Hill in Ipswich, Massachusetts. This 59-room Georgian mansion was equipped with ten bathrooms, each one beautifully decorated in soft-hued Italian marble. State-of-the-art plumbing and sterling silver fixtures finished off Crane's luxurious facilities.

The Great House has ten bathrooms, each one decorated with marble and sterling silver fixtures.

The Great House was designed to reflect the grand residences of England during the seventeenth century. It overlooks a magnificent grand allee, a ½-mile-long and 160-foot-wide area of well-groomed lawn that sweeps down to the sea. The interior of the

house features a 63-foot-long gallery with a 16-foot ceiling, dramatic circular staircase, library with ornamental wood carvings by seventeenth-century English craftsmen, bedrooms with panels shipped piece by piece from the London residence of William Hogarth and many other outstanding appointments.

The house is surrounded by a beautiful 1400-acre site (plus a 700-acre wildlife refuge) and, throughout the summer, concerts and festivals are held on the grounds.

Symphony under the Stars

On certain evenings throughout the summer months, The Great House's sweeping grand allee is transformed into one of the most elegant picnic spots in New England. Beginning in late afternoon, blankets and picnic baskets begin to cover the great expanse of green lawn that rolls down to the Atlantic Ocean. By 5 or 6 in the evening, music fills the air, and patrons are treated to a delightful concert under the stars.

The annual Independence Day Celebration in July, an all-American program of symphony music, Sousa marches, folk-singing and banjo-strumming, capped by fireworks over the ocean, is one of the favorite programs. Other concerts often include jazz, blues, reggae or Motown music.

The Concert Barn Series (some solo performances and small groups) runs from June through August and patrons are invited to picnic in the Tower Garden. Classical concerts (with champagne served during intermissions) are held in the fall, when activities are moved into the ballroom of The Great House. Private tours of the museum rooms are generally conducted from 6:30 to 7:30 for concertgoers.

Other special programs are held throughout the year, including annual events for children on Halloween and Christmas. Call 508-356-4351 for information and a schedule.

The General's Home

High Street
Thomaston, Maine
207-354-8062

OPEN:
Memorial Day–
Labor Day
Wed–Sun: 9–5:30
(last tour at 4:45)

ADMISSION:
Inquire for prices.

Montpelier

Thomaston, Maine
1931

Henry Knox was only 18 years old when he opened a bookshop in Boston and became one of his own best customers. He bought and read all the books he could get his hands on that had to do with military science. His shop soon became a gathering place for British officers stationed in Boston, and Knox spent many hours with them discussing military procedures.

He joined a local military company and, at the start of the Revolutionary War, was quick to join the American colonial army. Knox was to participate in nearly every important military engagement throughout the Revolution and, at its conclusion, was considered one of the most outstanding war heroes of his day.

One of his most spectacular feats of valor as colonel of artillery was transporting 60 tons of cannon and supplies more than 300 miles from Fort Ticonderoga (near the Canadian frontier) to Boston. These much-needed reinforcements, lashed to 42 ox-drawn sleighs, were slipped into Boston without detection. This resulted in a stunning victory for the patriots and the evacuation of British troops from Boston.

Following the war, Knox was made a major general and placed in command of West Point. In 1785, he was appointed Secretary of War under the presidency of George Washington. He served admirably in all his posts and retired from public life in 1794.

Knox chose Thomaston, Maine, as his retirement place. The first thing the general and his wife did was to build one of the most elegant homes ever seen in Maine. The imposing Federal-style three-story building was thought to be designed by Charles Bulfinch, but Knox himself specified many unusual details—an elliptical central facade, a completely oval front room

and a semi-flying staircase. The general and his wife, lavish entertainers, furnished the house with priceless antiques and furnishings.

Among the most celebrated furnishings in the house were several elegant pieces of furniture thought to have belonged to Marie Antoinette, the Queen of France. The story of how they got to their destination is quite a remarkable one.

At the time of the French Revolution, Captain Samuel Clough of nearby Wiscasset, Maine, was engaged in trade with France. While his ship, the *Sally*, was anchored in Paris awaiting cargo for the return voyage to America, he became involved with a plot to rescue the queen. A party of French sympathizers, aided by Lafayette, were working toward the liberation of many of the French nobility. King Louis XVI had already been beheaded, and it was feared (rightly so) that the queen would be next.

In preparation for sneaking the queen out of the country, it was arranged that her furnishings (said to be taken directly from the Tuileries but never verified) were to be smuggled aboard the *Sally*. The furniture was safely stowed away on board the boat, but Captain Clough waited in vain for the arrival of his

Montpelier was home to one of the most outstanding Revolutionary War heroes.

distinguished passenger. He soon learned that the plot to save her had been foiled and his own life was probably in danger. He quickly set sail for home port.

But what to do with his precious cargo? It is said that for many years he kept the furniture stored in his home near Wiscasset, not knowing what to do with it. Eventually, however, Clough decided to sell the furniture; several pieces were purchased by General Knox for his new home.

Knox died in 1806 (according to his son, "His death was occasioned by swallowing a chicken bone, which caused a mortification") and by this time his unsuccessful business ventures had cost him most of his wealth. Mrs. Knox continued to live in the mansion

Made in Maine—in Prison

Thomaston, Maine, is a small town situated on the banks of the St. George and Mill rivers. Visitors hurrying through it on busy Route 1 on their way to more glamorous spots such as Camden (home to the windjammers) or Booth Bay Harbor (one of Maine's premier summer resorts) hardly give Thomaston a second look. Little has changed here in the last century, and most of the buildings and houses along its main street still retain the flavor of the nineteenth century.

One of the buildings facing Main Street, however, stands out among the rest—it is a Maine state prison. And just a little farther down the street is one of the busiest spots in town, the Maine State Prison Showroom Outlet. Here, in a large warehouse, a fantastic assortment of handmade products is for sale—all made by prison inmates. Furniture, including desks, cedar chests, hutches, tables and chairs in many styles and sizes, are among the most popular items. Some are quite rustic; others are highly polished. Many pieces have a nautical theme, particularly sea chests and ship-wheel mirrors. Children's furniture and toys are in good supply and other hot sellers include T-shirts and sweatshirts with humorous slogans, such as the popular "Stolen from Maine State Prison." There are many games and novelty items, all are sturdily built and everything is very reasonably priced. Next time you are passing through Thomaston, be sure to take a second look. For more information call 207-354-2535.

until her death in 1824; for the next 30 years her two daughters occupied the sadly deteriorating house. When the last child died in 1854, the furnishings were auctioned off to pay family debts and the house was torn down to make way for the Knox and Lincoln Railroad.

In the early 1900s, the local chapter of the Daughters of the American Revolution began a campaign to raise money to erect a monument to the illustrious General Knox. Aided by a large contribution from the famous publisher and philanthropist Cyrus H. K. Curtis, they decided to build an exact replica of the general's former home. Many of the original pieces of furniture were either contributed or purchased back to fill the "new" Montpelier and to present, as nearly as possible, a sense of the lifestyle of the Knox family. One of the most outstanding pieces of furniture is the "original" mirror-fronted bookcase said to have come from the Tuileries.

The home is now administered by the State of Maine Bureau of Parks and Recreation Department and it is quite an impressive monument to one of Maine's most famous residents.

Henry Wadsworth Longfellow, his wife Frances and their sons Charles and Ernest.

Literary Landmarks

Nook Farm, a small neighborhood in Hartford, Connecticut, was a bucolic place in the mid-nineteenth century. It was here that an unusual group of outstanding writers and intellectuals of the day built their homes and lived together in a self-contained, close-knit community. Residents picked flowers from the colorful gardens of Harriet Beecher Stowe. In the evening, there was often a call across the lawn from Mark Twain's house to take part, along with his children and other guests, in an impromptu performance of "The Prince and the Pauper." And when Susan B. Anthony and Elizabeth Cady Stanton, the two leaders of the woman suffragist movement, were in town, there were lively discussions at Isabella Beecher Hooker's house just next door.

Hartford, by 1820, was the center of the publishing business in this country and more books were being published here at that time than in any other city in the United States. Many publishing firsts had already occurred here—the first American cookbook, the first American dictionary and speller (by Noah Webster) and the idea for magazine subscriptions.

The occupants of Nook Farm—free thinkers, champions of new ideas and social causes—had a wealth of material to contribute to keep the Hartford presses humming. They also attracted a large gathering of vistors to their little community—people distinguished in politics, education, literature, the arts and philanthropy. Quite naturally, the exchange of ideas and the interaction between such a highly gifted group was bound to bring the community a certain amount of everlasting fame.

The names of some of the residents (William Gillette, playwright and actor; Isabella Beecher Hooker, women's rights leader; Charles Dudley Warner, author and editor) have all but faded into obscurity. But two names, Harriet Beecher Stowe and Mark Twain, left an indelible mark on American literature.

Nook Farm is only one of the many areas in New England where writers have gathered over the years to live, meet and share their ideas. The writers of Concord, Massachusetts, the first "intellectual rebels" of New England—Emerson, Thoreau, Hawthorne and the Alcotts—all lived within a short distance of one another. Today there are at least a half-dozen houses (open to the public) of these and other former authors who lived near each other, and all are fascinating to visit.

Today, Nook Farm is a collection of distinct and unusual old Victorian buildings, surrounded by beautifully landscaped lawns, tall shade trees and flowering shrubs. This oasis of the nineteenth century is located in the heart of Hartford's bustling insurance industry. Gone are the shouts and laughter and spellbinding oratory of those early intellectuals who made their homes here, but their houses have been carefully preserved.

The House That Mark Built

Mark Twain House
Hartford, Connecticut
1874

351 Farmington
Avenue
Hartford, Conn.
203-525-9317

OPEN:
Year-round
Tues–Sat: 9:30–4
Sun: 12–4
June 1–
Columbus Day
Mon: 12–4
Closed holidays.

ADMISSION:
Inquire for prices.

To us, our house was not unsentient matter—it had a heart, and a soul, and eyes to see us with; and approvals, and solicitudes, and deep sympathies; it was of us, and we were in the peace of its benediction. We never came home from an absence that its face did not light up and speak out its eloquent welcome—and we could not enter it unmoved.

Mark Twain (né Samuel Langhorne Clemens), the author who wrote these lines, was an indefatigable traveler and lecturer. He delighted audiences around the world with his sharp wit and keen sense of humor. *The Adventures of Tom Sawyer* and *The Adventures of Huckleberry Finn* won him the distinction of being considered the first major author of American literature. It is little wonder that his massive wood and brick house, built in 1874—and the centerpiece of Nook Farm today—reflects his expansive personality. It has been compared to a giant cuckoo clock, a description that would not displease the humorist.

The house has a multi-turreted roofline with elaborate overhangs and balconies. Yards of "stick-style" railings surround the brilliantly painted black and vermilion exterior. The exterior bricks change angles, directions and projections, creating patterns and designs reminiscent of the Native Americans of the Southwest. In a poem entitled "This is the House That Mark Built," Twain wrote:

These are the bricks of various hue
And shape and position, straight and askew,
With the nooks and angles and gables too,
Which make up the house presented to view,
The curious house that Mark built.

The Indian basketweave design is carried into the enormous entrance hall, where his children's birthday parties were held. The ornately carved black walnut woodwork has panel insets stenciled in silver, and the ceilings and upper walls are painted in terracotta with dark blue patterns designed by Louis Comfort Tiffany.

The library is evocative of the Victorian love of clutter. Although Twain claimed this room gave him a spirit of deep contentment, the bright Oriental carpeting, heavy red velvet draperies, blue-and-gold wallpaper (covering both ceiling and walls) and colorful array of knickknacks is more apt to prompt a feeling of utter confusion.

The third floor of the house was where Twain wrote in his little study, entertained his friends in the billiards room and walked out onto his high balcony and pretended he was back piloting a Mississippi River steamboat. But his favorite room was his bedroom. Dominating the room is an elaborately hand-carved bed in which Twain (who stayed in bed every morning until at least 10 A.M.) liked to lie—with his

" . . . The curious house that Mark built."

head at the footboard—gazing at the intricate carvings on the headboard. Each of the bedposts supports an almost life-size cherub. An extension cord from the chandelier to the bedpost was within easy reach of the author, who often woke up at night and wrote down an idea for a story.

Twain was a loving father and husband, but had very strict, rigid ideas about women. He saw no reason for his three daughters to be subjected to math and science—it was "unfit" for girls—so his children were educated at home by their mother. Their nursery is filled with a wonderful collection of toys and furniture; the wallpaper, designed by Walter Crane, an English artist and illustrator, whimsically depicts scenes from "Ye Frog He Would A-Wooing Go."

The basement of the house has been turned into a museum. It contains papers and memorabilia of Twain's, including his antique typewriter and the cause of his greatest financial loss, the Paige typesetter. Twain was the first author to submit a typewritten manuscript to a publisher and he was intrigued by the potential of machines, such as a typesetter, which could speed the process of writing. He invested heavily in the Paige typesetter, which was intended to revolutionize the printing business. But the machine only succeeded in bankrupting its investors. Twain lost almost $300,000 on the machine. Coupled with the failure of other poor investments, he was forced to close his home in 1893 and set out on a year-long lecture tour to pay his debts.

He was able to recoup his losses, but great personal tragedies kept him from ever returning to his Hartford home again. While in Europe, he received the news that his oldest and most favored daughter, Suzy, was gravely ill. She had been staying with friends, but when she became ill she was taken to the family home. It was there that she died of spinal meningitis. Mrs. Clemens never got over her grief from the loss of her daughter. Upon returning from Europe, she refused to return to the Hartford house.

"The spirits of the dead hallow a house for me,"

wrote Twain in 1911. "Suzy died in the house we built in Hartford. Mrs. Clemens would never enter it again. But it made the house dearer to me. I visited it once since; when it was tenantless and forlorn, but to me it was a holy place and beautiful."

Thanks to the Mark Twain Memorial, the house is still "hallowed," and rings with the happy echo of the man and his family who so loved and enjoyed this place.

Is This the Party to Whom I am Speaking?

Mark Twain, usually fascinated with new inventions, had little use for the telephone. Shortly after Kate Leary came to work for the Clemens as Mrs. Clemens' maid, she reported the following incident:

One night Mrs. Taft, the wife of Dr. Taft (lovely people that lived in Hartford), she called him up and George [the Butler] answered the telephone first and then he went and called Mr. Clemens. So Mr. Clemens went out to speak to her but he didn't know who was at the telephone, so he said "Hello! Hello!" He thought it was one of them hello girls [telephone operators]. Mrs. Taft didn't answer him quick enough, so he says, very loud, What in —— the matter with you down there? Are you all asleep? Why, he was so mad by then, he didn't even hear Mrs. Taft, and he kept shouting, "If I don't get better service than this I am going to have this pulled right out of my house, if I don't get any better service from you hello girls down there!"

He was swearing and carrying on something awful, so Mrs. Clemens heard him and opened the dining-room door and put her finger up to her lips. Then, of course, he quieted down and poor Mrs. Taft had a chance to be heard at last! So she says very polite:

"Good evening, Mr. Clemens."

"Oh," he says, "Is this you, Mrs. Taft? Well," he says, "well, well! I just this minute come to the telephone! George has been trying to talk, and he's been having such a bad time with this old telephone, I had to come and help him and see what I could do!"

—From *A Lifetime with Mark Twain, the memories of Katy Leary, for thirty years his Faithful and Devoted Servant* by Mary Lawton (New York: Harcourt Brace and Co., 1912).

Good Neighbors

The Harriet Beecher Stowe House

Hartford, Connecticut
1871

77 Forest Street
Hartford, Conn.
203-525-9317

OPEN:
Year-round
Tues–Sat: 9:30–4
Sun: 12–4

June 1–
Columbus Day
Mon: 12–4

Closed holidays.

ADMISSION:
Inquire for prices.

The former home of Harriet Beecher Stowe, just across the lawn from the Mark Twain House, has a quiet, almost sedate look to it, reflecting the author's personality. Harriet's literary career began as a means to supplement her husband's meager salary. Calvin Stowe was a professor of biblical studies and, with seven children to support, there was barely enough money to cover their debts.

With the publication of *Uncle Tom's Cabin* in 1852, however, the Stowes' financial position was greatly changed. The book sold more then 1½ million copies the first year, and was eventually translated into 40 languages. While the publication of this book made her the most famous and well-paid writer in the country, it did not affect her character in any way. She continued to write in a businesslike manner, always feeling the need to provide more security for her large family. Her other works, spanning more than 50 years, include more than 30 books—novels, biographies, poetry, nonfiction and children's stories.

In 1869, Harriet and her sister Catharine wrote a popular book called *The American Woman's Home.* This book set the trend for the interior decoration of many homes in America at the time. The present kitchen of the Stowe house has been restored following the design illustrated in her book, showing all the practical time-saving methods put to use by the two sisters. Many of their designs for efficient kitchen tools are all neatly displayed.

If you visit the Harriet Beecher Stowe House in spring or summer, you will enjoy the profusion of color from the old-fashioned flower gardens completely surrounding the house. Bright splashes of vibrant colors set off against the simple building keep

the illusion that Harriet, who had a passion for flowers, still lives there and tends the gardens. The house's buff-colored brick walls are neatly set off by cocoa brown wood trim and moss-green painted shutters. Several small gables all properly placed in the steep hip roof add to an overall tidy appearance.

Inside the house, nostalgic Victorian bouquets of fresh flowers can be found in every room. There is a light, airy feeling. No dark Victorian over-drapes are to be found here. There are, in fact, few curtains at all—a rash departure from the style of the day. Mrs. Stowe decorated her large windows with ivy and potted plants to let in as much sunlight as possible and to provide a full view of her lovely flower gardens.

The house is decorated throughout with many personal belongings of the family. Included is the mahogany drop-leaf table on which she wrote her famous novel, *Uncle Tom's Cabin*, which has been credited with changing forever the American attitude toward slavery. She was an accomplished painter in both oils and watercolors, and many of her original artworks are on display. One small table holds a china tea set that she designed. In a little sitting room just off her second-floor bedroom, where she did most of her writing, rest several pieces of furniture, all hand-painted and decorated by the author. This was the room where Harriet would write for three hours each day, surrounded by her own craftsmanship.

The Stowes spent many happy years at Nook Farm and fully enjoyed the open exchange of hospitality with their distinguished neighbors. Harriet died at Nook Farm in 1896, outliving her husband and five of her children. In 1924, her grand-niece, Katharine Seymour Day, purchased the house and set up the Stowe-Day foundation, which now manages the house.

Vintage Hartford

The Old State House in downtown Hartford is the oldest in the nation. It was designed by renowned architect Charles Bulfinch and built sometime between 1792 and 1796. It served as the seat of Connecticut's state government from 1796 to 1878 and then became Hartford's city hall from 1879 to 1915. It has been restored in recent years and is now a museum with changing exhibits, period rooms, gift shops and a visitor center. The multi-windowed senate chambers, with its large Gilbert Stuart portrait of George Washington, is quite impressive. Guided tours are given (call ahead) and outdoor concerts and farmers' markets are held here in season. For more information call 203-522-6766.

The Wadsworth Atheneum, the nation's oldest public art museum, is also located in downtown Hartford and ranks high among art critics. It, too, has undergone recent extensive renovations, making more gallery space for its permanent collection of more than 45,000 art objects. On display are changing exhibits of treasures from ancient Egyptian artifacts to contemporary sculpture. The Wallace Nutting Collection, one of the largest and best-known collections of Colonial American furniture dating from 1630 to 1730, is of particular interest. The Lions Gallery of the Senses has exhibits for the visually impaired. For information call 203-247-9111 or 203-278-2670.

227 South Main
Street
West Hartford,
Conn.
203-521-5362

OPEN:
Year-round
Mon–Thurs: 10–4
Sun: 1–4

ADMISSION:
Inquire for prices.

The Noah Webster House

West Hartford, Connecticut
1 7 4 8

I have contributed in a small degree to the instruction of at least four million of the rising generation; and it is not unreasonable to expect that a few seeds of improvement, planted by my hand, may germinate and grow and ripen into valuable fruit when my remains shall be mingled with the dust.

The birthplace and boyhood home of Noah Webster is several miles west of Nook Farm. This eighteenth-century house in West Hartford is a memorial to the man known as the "schoolmaster to America."

Webster was born in 1758 and lived in this house until he entered Yale. He went on to become a schoolteacher, lawyer, editor, legislator, lecturer and one of the founders of Amherst College in Massachusetts. He wrote on many subjects and, because many of his books were freely copied, he instigated and created some of the first American copyright laws.

Webster's famous *Blue-Backed Speller,* which helped standardize American spelling and pronunciation, spread across the continent in the late 1700s. Even western pioneer families taught their children to read from it. He authored the American Dictionary which, in its numerous editions, has outsold every book in the English language except the Bible. For centuries, children have been taught to "look it up in Webster's."

In 1828, at the age of 70 years, Webster completed his monumental work on the dictionary. He wrote:

When I had come to the last word, I was seized with a trembling which made it somewhat difficult to hold my pen steady for writing. The cause seems to have been the thought that I might not then live to finish the work, or the thought that I was so near the end of my labors.

Webster's two-story frame house with red painted clapboards dates from around 1748, with major additions completed in 1749 and 1787. It has been restored with the simple furnishings of a typical eighteenth-century farmhouse. Schoolchildren who visit here from many surrounding towns are introduced to what life was like for young boys and girls growing up during that period.

The home of Noah Webster, the author of the American dictionary.

Authentically costumed guides lead tours, and everyone participates in hands-on activities, including fireplace cooking, bread baking, butter churning, spinning, weaving, exploring the herb gardens and chicken coop and engaging in role-playing. Children learn about Noah's father, who was a weaver as well as a farmer. Tour guides tell interesting stories—such as why the word "spinster" was derived from the spinning wheel—as they help visitors try the related tasks.

The house is always bustling with activity, and teachers and instructors are unanimous in their praise of the experiences children are exposed to at the Noah Webster House. It is a fitting tribute to the man who planted "a few seeds of improvement."

A Penny Saved . . .

The town of Simsbury is just north of West Hartford and is a town of many firsts. The first copper coins were struck here after copper was discovered in Simsbury in 1705. The first steel mill in America was in Simsbury and began operating in 1744. The first temperance society in the country—The Aquatics—was established in town. And the manufacture of the first safety fuse in America originated in Simsbury in 1836.

Exhibits highlighting all these firsts can be seen at Massacoh Plantation, a complex of buildings representing three centuries of local history. Among the buildings that make up Massacoh Plantation are the 1771 Captain Elisha Phelps House (his younger brother, Noah, was the first spy of the Revolutionary War), a replica of the 1683 Meeting House (built in 1969 for Simsbury's 1970 Tercentenary), the 1795 Hendricks Cottage (home of Timothy Woodbridge, who was one of the men who struck the first copper "Higley pennies"), a 1740 schoolhouse and a fuse-manufacturing shop. Call 203-658-2500 for information.

The Henry Wadsworth Longfellow House

Cambridge, Massachusetts
1759

105 Brattle Street
Cambridge, Mass.
617-876-4491

OPEN:
Year-round
Daily 10–4:30 (last tour at 4)
Closed major holidays

ADMISSION:
Inquire for prices.

The home of Henry Wadsworth Longfellow is a handsome Georgian-style house on Brattle Street in Cambridge, Massachusetts. Its history predates Longfellow, though—Major John Vassall lived here before the Revolution, and was forced to flee the country on the eve of the Revolution. George Washington was quartered here during the siege of Boston. He and Martha not only entertained many important visitors in the house but also celebrated their seventeenth wedding anniversary in the large parlor on the first floor.

What has made it a National Landmark and one of the most visited houses in New England is that it was home to Longfellow, one of America's most celebrated poets. In 1837, the house was given to Longfellow and his new bride, Fanny Appleton, as a wedding present from Fanny's father. Longfellow was to live here for the next 45 years.

The Longfellows spent many happy years in this house and it was here that he wrote most of his immortal poems, including "The Wreck of the Hesperus," "The Midnight Ride of Paul Revere" and "The Children's Hour." Visitors have been known to stand in the front hall and recite whole stanzas from these poems, especially the lines:

From my study I see in the lamplight,
descending the broad hall stair,
grave Alice, and laughing Allegra,
and Edith with golden hair.

But it was also here that Longfellow suffered the greatest tragedy of his life, the death of his beloved wife. On a hot July day in 1861, Fanny Longfellow sat at a little desk by an open window in the study. She was wearing a light, gauzy dress of fine muslin. A lighted candle for melting sealing wax stood on the desk and, as she bent to seal a small packet containing a lock of hair from one of her children, the sleeve of her dress brushed the flame. In an instant she was engulfed in fire.

In panic she ran from the study to the room across the hall where her husband sat reading. At the sight of her in flames, he sprang to his feet and, pulling a rug from the floor, threw it around her to quell the flames. He held her in his arms, protecting her face and as much of her body as possible as he extinguished the fire.

His efforts, however, were in vain. Her burns were fatal, and she died the next morning. Her funeral a few days later was on the anniversary of their wedding day.

Longfellow, severely burned on the face and hands, was too ill to attend her funeral. So deep was his grief over the loss of his beloved wife that it would be 18 more years before he could put his feelings into

Henry Wadsworth Longfellow, in his study.

words. He penned a beautiful sonnet, "The Cross of Snow," but the poem was hidden away in his desk and not discovered until after his death in 1882.

Such is the cross I wear upon my breast these eighteen years, through all the changing scenes and seasons, changeless since the day she died.

The Longfellow House is owned and maintained by the National Park Service. The furnishings are all original to the house, and they maintain the ambiance of the 45 years that the Longfellows resided here.

Tory Row

Stretching along Brattle Street in Cambridge is a row of handsome eighteenth-century houses built in colonial days by a group of wealthy merchants. Most of the occupants were Tories, loyal to the Crown, and the street was eventually to become known as "Tory Row." On the eve of the Revolution, the owners were forced to flee Cambridge, never to return. The deserted houses were soon occupied by officers of the Continental Army. General Washington himself occupied the 1759 house of a noted Tory, Major John Vassall.

Two of the houses are now open to the public. The first, the Vassall House, is best known for its last occupant—Henry Wadsworth Longfellow. It is furnished much as it was when the poet and his family lived there, including many of Longfellow's personal mementos, such as his desk and writing implements. The Hooper-Lee-Nichols House, one of the oldest houses in Cambridge, is now headquarters to the Cambridge Historical Society. It was built by Dr. Richard Hooper, then occupied by noted Tory merchant Judge Joseph Lee and later by wealthy merchant George Nichols. Some of the rooms are furnished with period pieces; others illustrate the various architectural details of several different building periods.

At the foot of Brattle Street is The Blacksmith House, which was made famous by Longfellow's poem "The Village Blacksmith." It was built in 1727 for loyalist William Brattle, who gave the street its name. It is now home to the Cambridge Center for Adult Education and has a pastry shop and café. Call 617-354-3036 for information.

The Secret Staircase

54 Turner Street
Salem, Mass.
508-744-0991

OPEN:
Year-round
Daily: 10–4

July 1–Labor Day
Daily: 9:30–5:30

Closed Jan. 1,
Thanksgiving and
Christmas.

ADMISSION:
Inquire for prices.

The House of the Seven Gables

Salem, Massachusetts
1668

Half-way down a by-street of one of our New England towns stands a rusty wooden house, with seven acutely peaked gables, facing towards various points of the compass, and a huge, clustered chimney in the midst . . . The aspect of the venerable mansion has always affected me like a human countenance bearing the traces not merely of outward storm and sunshine, but expressive, also, of the long lapse of mortal life, and accompanying vicissitudes that have passed within.

So begins Nathaniel Hawthorne's classic novel, *The House of the Seven Gables.* And so intricately is this house in Salem, Massachusetts, identified with his novel that it is often difficult to separate historical fact from Hawthorne's fiction.

Hawthorne was born in Salem in 1804 and lived there until 1850. As a youth, he was intrigued by his older cousin, Susannah Ingersoll, and her great, dark, brooding house overlooking Salem harbor. He visited her there often, and together they explored the house. One of their favorite spots was the attic, where they could trace the outlines of the gables (there were only three on the house at that time). When they discovered the stubbled remains of four more gables, Hawthorne was said to have uttered in great delight, "The House of the *Seven* Gables—that sounds well."

Susannah also told Hawthorne about Salem's history and the part their ancestors played in it. Major William Hathorne (as the family name was then spelled) was among the first settlers in Salem in 1630, and one of the most ruthless persecutors of the Quakers. One of those who suffered severely at his hands was John Maule. Later, the major's son, Colonel John Hathorne, was one of the judges in the infamous

witch trials, and it is said that one of the accused, Matthew Maule, put a curse on the judges, saying "God will give you blood to drink."

The inspiration for Hawthorne's famous novel, *The House of the Seven Gables.*

Many years later, in writing *The House of the Seven Gables*, Hawthorne used this curse as the basis for his romantic tale of several generations of the fictional Pyncheon family who inhabit the house and the perils that befall them.

Visitors to the house invariably attempt to identify each gable as it relates to the novel. Upon entering the house, they are further entertained by spotting such well-known plot themes as Hepzibah's cent shop, the Judge's chair, Phoebe's chamber and Clifford's room. But one of the most fascinating features of the house for visitors, and one that is only hinted at in the story, is the secret staircase.

"The deep projection of the second story gave the house such a meditative look that you could not pass it without the idea that it had secrets to keep and an eventful history to moralize upon," wrote Hawthorne. And indeed, the secret staircase, built behind the wood storage closet next to the fireplace in the dining room, remains a mystery to this day. It has caused a good deal of speculation on the part of both historians and Hawthorne readers.

It is thought that the secret staircase dates back to the original family that built the house, the Turners. Captain John Turner was a prosperous merchant and shipowner trading in Barbados, and he and his descendents who lived in the house were leading citizens of Salem for three generations. But why would Turner have built this hidden passageway?

There are two theories. During the Salem witch trials, hardly any family was spared the worry of being accused of witchcraft. The Turners may have planned to use the staircase as a hiding place should one of their members be so accused. The second theory is that Turner might have been trading in illegal goods, and used the staricase to aid his smuggling operation.

Susannah Ingersoll died in 1858. Subsequent owners of the house did not know of the secret staircase until 1883. Men working on the old chimney were quite surprised to find it, as were the owners. They also found, on one of the stairs, a pine tree sixpence and a very old book, thought to be a prayer book or a hymn book, with an inscription inside: "Cuffy his book." (Cuffy also remains a mystery to this day.)

In *The House of the Seven Gables*, Hawthorne only alludes to the mysterious way in which Clifford appears in the dining room, so frightening Judge Pyncheon that the judge is seized by a "stroke of apoplexy" and dies. The fact that Hawthorne does not tell how Clifford gets from his second-floor bedroom to the dining room—and does not mention such a fascinating subject as a secret staircase—continues to puzzle readers and visitors alike.

Many believe that Susannah Ingersoll asked Hawthorne not to mention the secret staircase in the book. Although she was considered to be a recluse, it is known that she was an advocate of abolition and secretly active in the Underground Railroad—perhaps hiding escaped slaves in the stairway. Hawthorne, to prevent scandal, would have heeded her wishes.

In the early 1900s, the house, which had become

very run-down and neglected, was purchased and completely restored to its original design—including the seven gables—by Caroline O. Emmerton, a philanthropist from a well-known Salem family. Miss Emmerton had become interested in the Settlement House movement, a reaction to the harsh labor laws of early-twentieth-century England. Centers—settlement houses—were established in underprivileged neighborhoods to provide services to those in need. Miss Emmerton purchased the House of Seven Gables with the idea of restoring it as Hawthorne described it in his novel, then opening it up to the public to raise money for a settlement house.

Today the House of the Seven Gables is part of a complex of several other seventeenth-century Salem houses that have been moved to this location and restored; one of these houses is the birthplace of Nathaniel Hawthorne. The complex is owned and operated by The House of the Seven Gables Settlement Association.

The Witch House

This house is more properly known as the Jonathan Corwin House, but because it and its owner were so closely involved in the infamous witch trials, it is popularly called the Witch House. In 1692, during the Salem witchcraft trials, it was the home of Judge Jonathan Corwin. Corwin, along with another magistrate, John Hathorne (who lived in the House of the Seven Gables), presided over preliminary hearings and interrogated more than 200 of the accused in this house.

The house is very similar in appearance to the House of the Seven Gables. Its dark shingles, diamond-paned casements, steep gables and second-story overhang give the house a sinister appearance—just the way one would expect a witch's house to look.

The house was built about 1642, then remodeled by Corwin in 1675. Kept in his family for several generations, it is now managed by the Salem Parks Department. It is furnished with many fine seventeenth-century period pieces. For information, call 508-744-0180.

Edith Wharton at her desk in the library of The Mount.

Dramatic Domiciles

Many of the old New England houses have served as backdrops for various theatrical events. Some of them have been featured in both classic and modern films and are instantly recognizable in such productions as "The House of the Seven Gables," "The Victorians" and "The Great Gatsby."

The houses included in this chapter are not film stars, but ones that in some way have made their own contribution to the world of entertainment. Visitors are often surprised to find these houses—whose quiet exteriors belie their dramatic past—tucked away in small farming communities and sedate little villages.

Other houses, such as The Mount in Lenox, Massachusetts, or The Monte Cristo Cottage in New London, Connecticut, continue to play an important part in current theater productions.

A Real-Life Setting

325 Pequot Avenue
New London, Conn.
203-443-0051

OPEN:
April 1–
December 21
Mon–Fri: 10–5

ADMISSION:
Inquire for prices.

The Monte Cristo Cottage

New London, Connecticut

1888

Probably no other house in America has played such a significant role in American literature as the home of one of the country's greatest playwrights, Eugene O'Neill. His two most highly acclaimed works, *Long Day's Journey Into Night* and *Ah, Wilderness!* took as their setting his boyhood home in New London, Connecticut. It was named Monte Cristo Cottage by his father, the actor James O'Neill, who was celebrated throughout his life for his most famous role, that of the Count of Monte Cristo.

Much has been written by drama critics and scholars of the irony of these two plays by O'Neill—one his greatest tragedy, and the other his only comedy. Both chronicle the same period of the young playwright's life when he was growing up in New London. While *Long Day's Journey Into Night* is completely autobiographical, showing the dark, true side of O'Neill's life, *Ah, Wilderness!* is a light-hearted comedy of domestic bliss—and pure fantasy. O'Neill once explained the latter play by saying, "The truth is that I had no youth. *Ah, Wilderness!* was nostalgia for a youth I never had."

In both plays, particularly *Long Day's Journey Into Night*, O'Neill describes the house in meticulous detail. This has caused an interesting phenomenon. Actors and actresses who have starred in O'Neill's plays have felt lured to the real-life setting of this drama. In fact, many of them have made pilgrimages to this small cottage by the sea to draw inspiration and understanding from it.

Geraldine Fitzgerald, Colleen Dewhurst, Helen Hayes, Katherine Hepburn, Jason Robards, Jr., Jack Lemmon, Liv Ullman, Robert Redford, Glenda Jackson and Siobhan McKenna are only a few of the stars who have visited the house. Jason Robards, Jr., considered the principal acting exponent of O'Neill in America, has been to the house many times. He and Geraldine Fitzgerald once did a scene from *Long Day's Journey Into Night* in the front room.

Curator Sally Pavetti has met all these actors and actresses, and calls Jason Robards "an old friend." She has many stories to tell about the different reactions her guests feel when they walk through the house. "Many of them claim to feel the presence of the family in this house," she says, "which has helped them in their interpretation of their roles." Most of the actresses who play Mary Tyrone, the drug-addicted mother, are quite emotional about the tower room. According to Sally, "They want to feel what it's like to be Mrs. O'Neill. I think mothers more than anybody else feel that way."

The house stood abandoned for many years after the deaths of O'Neill's parents. It was purchased by a

Monte Cristo, the boyhood home of Eugene O'Neill.

private owner in 1937 and later, in 1971, declared a National Landmark. At that time it was sold to the Eugene O'Neill Theater Center. Its popularity as a cultural attraction and educational resource has steadily increased over the years.

O'Neill also used locations in and around New London for the settings of his other plays—*Mourning Becomes Electra, Desire Under the Elms, A Moon for the Misbegotten,* and *The Great God Brown.* But the Monte Cristo Cottage is the one that lives on in O'Neill's works.

New London Honors O'Neill

Eugene O'Neill's boyhood in New London had a lasting influence on his life. Although he had few good things to say about the city in his later years, it is obvious to all who read his plays that it is this place more than anywhere else that shaped his life.

While not a native son (he was born in New York City in 1888), he came here as an infant with his family in the summer of 1888 and continued to spend his summers here until 1919. He is very much treated like a native son by the city of New London, however, and on the 100th anniversary of his birth in 1988, an elaborate city-wide celebration—complete with a gala ball, band concerts and fireworks—was held. Also in honor of the event, a statue of O'Neill was commissioned to be placed in a new park at City Pier. The statue was inspired by a photo of O'Neill at about the age of eight or nine, sitting on a rock in front of the family cottage.

Another great tribute to O'Neill is the Eugene O'Neill Theater Center (actually situated on the edge of town in Waterford) that has become internationally known for promoting new works for the American theater. Stage readings of new plays and musicals are presented in July and August. Call 203-443-5378 for schedule and information.

The Great American Songbird

Nordica Homestead

Farmington, Maine

1840

Holly Road
Farmington, Maine
207-778-2042

OPEN:
June 1–Labor Day
Tues–Sun: 10–12
and 1–5

ADMISSION:
Inquire for prices.

Lillian Nordica, née Lily Norton, was once known in every corner of the world as "The Great American Songbird." She was born in 1857 in a simple little farmhouse in the small village of Farmington, Maine. While Lily was still a small child, her parents recognized the superior quality of her sweet soprano voice (later referred to as "a voice of liquid purity, exceptional range and magnificent power"). They sent her to study at the New England Conservatory of Music in Boston, where she impressed her teachers not only with her beautiful voice but with her willingness to work hard at her lessons.

Lily made her operatic debut at age 22 in Italy. She was such a tremendous hit with the Italians that they nicknamed her *la Giglia Nordica* ("Lily of the North"). She soon adopted the title "Madame Nordica" for her stage name.

From Italy she went on to sing in every great opera house in the world, performing a wide variety of roles and winning many honors. In 1911, at the height of her career, she toured the United States in her own luxurious private railroad car (named "Brunnhilde" after one of her most famous operatic roles), giving 60 concerts in 50 cities. The last city, in which she gave perhaps her most memorable performance, was her hometown of Farmington. Though she had sung before all the crowned heads of Europe, she never forgot her humble beginnings, nor her friends and neighbors back home.

The much-heralded performance was held at a local state college, which had the only auditorium large enough to accommodate the crowd that wanted to attend. Lily did not disappoint her hometown. Adorned in complete regalia, including jewels and a

Lillian Nordica in her
famous role as
Brunnhilde.

diamond tiara, she sang her most celebrated operatic
roles as though she were performing in Carnegie Hall
or London's Covent Garden. The appreciative specta-
tors greeted her with thunderous applause at the end
of each number. When she concluded her concert
with a simple rendition of "Home, Sweet Home," her
raptured audience rose as one, applauding and weep-
ing at the same time.

Two years later, halfway through a round-the-
world tour, Lily had a premonition of her death. After
a particularly brilliant performance at the opera

house in Sydney, Australia, she suddenly announced to her accompanist and friend, E. Romayne Simmons, "I shall never sing another note."

He was startled by such an absurd remark, but gave it little attention, assuming that the famous soprano was suffering from a temporary case of fatigue. But two days later, while aboard a boat that was transporting her to the next stop on her tour, Lily developed a cold. During the night the boat ran aground on a reef in the Coral Seas, and the passengers were forced to sleep on the open deck for several days before being rescued. By this time, Lily's cold had developed into pneumonia. She had to be brought ashore on a stretcher to a small island with few medical facilities. The authorities sent to the

---

Living History

Not far from Nordica Homestead, in Livermore, Maine, is Norlands, a living history center. A year-round working farm with oxen, horses, sheep, cows and crops, it also offers visitors a unique hands-on approach to history by experiencing rural life as it was lived in northern New England in the nineteenth century.

Norlands is the former home of the extraordinary Washburn family, whose lives greatly influenced American history. The seven sons of Israel and Patty Washburn, born here in the early 1800s, grew up to be governors, senators, ambassadors and cabinet members. Four were members of Congress from various states—three of them simultaneously.

The farm is composed of five century-old buildings—school, library, church, the Washburn House with attached farmer's cottage, barn—and 430 acres of farmland and woodland. Participants come here for two- and three-night stays to take part in all aspects of farm life, from cooking on a wood stove to pitching hay in the fields. There is also time for social events such as a husking bee or a quilting party—and there's always fresh-made ice cream for dessert.

The program is especially popular with teachers and museum educators, but participation is open to all adults. There is also a special one-day program for children. For information call 207-897-2236.

mainland for a cow so that Madame Nordica could have fresh milk.

Marooned for almost three months on this remote and ill-equipped island, and with Lily's health deteriorating, Simmons had to threaten the steamship company with blackmail to get Madame Nordica and her entourage moved to a more civilized place. A schooner was finally sent, and delivered them to Batavia, Java. Three weeks later, Madame Nordica died there. As she had forewarned her friend that night in Sydney, she had, indeed, sung her last note.

Several years after her death, friends and admirers of Lily formed the Nordica Memorial Association, raising money to purchase and restore Nordica Homestead, her birthplace. Meticulously restored and preserved, it houses a magnificent collection of Madame Nordica's operatic gowns and jewelry. It also contains many of the gifts she received from admirers, such as a heavily carved chair from Diamond Jim Brady and an elaborate teakwood console, a gift of the Emperor of China.

Mr. Fourth of July

Roseland Cottage
Woodstock, Connecticut
1846

On the Common
Route 169
Woodstock, Conn.
203-928-4074

OPEN:
Mid-May–
mid-September
Wed–Sun: 12–5

Mid-September–
mid-October
Fri–Sun: 12–5

ADMISSION:
Inquire for prices.

When it came to celebrating the nation's birthday, no one did it better than Henry C. Bowen. Beginning in the mid-1800s and continuing until his death in 1896, his annual star-spangled, skyrocketing Fourth of July party (reported in all the newspapers of the day as "the best this nation has ever known") took place in the quiet little country town of Woodstock, Connecticut. It was attended by a succession of United States presidents, from Grant to McKinley, as well as many noted celebrities of the day.

Bowen, born and educated in Woodstock, left his hometown at the age of 21 to seek his fortune in New York City. He became a successful silk merchant and, later, the owner of *The Independent*, a weekly journal that published outspoken views on the abolition of slavery. Throughout his life his strong character and patriotic zeal left a lasting impression on all.

He always thought of Woodstock as home. His large summer house—a salmon pink Gothic Revival mansion—stood in the center of town. He surrounded it with rose gardens and named it Roseland. All summer long he and his wife would entertain famous guests. Among his visitors were Oliver Wendell Holmes, Harriet Beecher Stowe, Rev. Henry Ward Beecher and, on more than one occasion, Julia Ward Howe. On one visit, Julia was rendered a tribute when the invited guests rose and sang her famous song, "The Battle Hymn of the Republic."

The early Fourth of July celebrations were held on the grounds of Roseland, but as the number of guests grew, Bowen extended the activities to the town green across the way. Eventually, he purchased land on the edge of town to create Roseland Park, which could accommodate the ever-growing crowd that

swarmed into town for this well-publicized event.

It was a wild and wonderful party that began at the crack of dawn and lasted well into the night. Red, white and blue flags and bunting flew from every porch, fence and flagpole in town. Bands played and church bells rang throughout the day. There were games and races for the children, stirring speeches for the adults, tons of strawberry shortcake and gallons of pink lemonade (prepared by the ladies of Woodstock) to be consumed by one and all.

At Roseland Cottage itself, the invited guests, often numbering as many as 500, would be treated to a lavish dinner prepared by expert chefs and caterers brought in from New York City for the occasion. No alcoholic beverages were served, however, as Bowen did not approve of drinking. And he didn't approve of smoking, either—at one party, as President Grant prepared to light up one of his famous cigars, Bowen promptly reminded him that he "did not permit its indulgence" in his home. With that, Grant excused himself and went outside to smoke.

Toward the end of the day, as the sun lowered behind the distant hills, the excitement reached a feverish pitch. In great anticipation, all eyes searched the sky. Finally, a spectacular, booming fireworks display would light up the night sky for miles around. The shouts and cheers from the crowd mingled with ear-piercing rockets and exploding Roman candles.

Bowen believed that the Fourth of July should be a day of public rejoicing, with waving flags, ringing bells, booming cannons, beating drums and trumpeting bugles. And he did his best to see that the nation's birthday was properly celebrated.

Woodstock has returned to being a quiet little country town these days. The salmon-pink mansion, now owned and operated by the Society for the Preservation of New England Antiquities, still stands in all its glory across from the town green. On the Fourth of July, its flag waves silently in the breeze. Gone now are the crowds and the cheers. But toward evening, just after sunset, some say you can still hear the soft echoes of those giant skyrockets and the hearty laughter of "Mr. Fourth of July" himself.

The Pink House

Most people driving through Woodstock for the first time are apt to gasp as they pass Roseland Cottage. The bright pink Gothic Revival mansion, richly ornamented and set off by formal gardens and manicured lawns, is quite spectacular.

It has become popularly known as "the pink house," and with good reason. Soon after the house was completed in 1846, a profusion of pink roses was planted around the house. The gardens, said to be the most beautiful in Windham County, prompted the owner of the house, Henry Bowen, to name it Roseland.

There are several outbuildings on the property. One of them contains one of the earliest private bowling alleys in the country. Another is a Classical-style garden house which is adjacent to the oldest known boxwood garden in New England.

The pink house remained in the Bowen family until the last descendant—Constance Holt, Bowen's granddaughter—died. Miss Holt was known to host "pink teas," using pink linens and china. Roseland is now operated by the Society for the Preservation of New England Antiquities, which strives to keep it in the pink!

Special events, teas and children's parties are held here throughout the summer. Call 203-928-4074 for schedules and information.

Drama in the Drawing Room

Plunkett Street
Lenox, Mass.
413-637-1899

OPEN:
May–October
Schedule changes
each year. Call for
exact days and
hours.

ADMISSION:
Inquire for prices.

The Mount

Lenox, Massachusetts
1902

Edith Wharton, considered one of America's foremost writers, wrote about her Berkshire summer home in her autobiography, *A Backward Glance*, "The Mount was my first real home . . . and its blessed influence still lives in me."

She would be pleased, no doubt, that her influence still lives on at The Mount. On summer afternoons, plays based on her writings are performed in her elegant drawing room, with tea served in the dining room during intermission. All plays are based on the writer's life work and the works of her friend and frequent guest, Henry James.

Prior to designing and building The Mount, Edith Wharton spent summers in Newport. Born to a rich and prominent family, she was expected to follow the conventional pattern for women of her day by marrying, having children and accepting the social responsibilities of women of her class. But Edith preferred to pursue a career as a writer. She would later write that old New York society viewed authorship "as something between a black art and a form of manual labor"—and certainly not something a proper young lady would do.

Her first successful book, *The Decoration of Houses*, was written with noted architect Ogden Codman. This book not only launched her career but allowed her to build a house which gave her the freedom she needed to become a professional writer. She designed a separate wing for herself at The Mount, consisting of a boudoir, bath and bedroom that could be closed off from the rest of the house—not only from family and friends, but from her husband as well.

Here in these private quarters, she set up a strict schedule for herself. Waking early in the morning, she would prop herself up on her pillows and, with pencil and pad in front of her, begin writing. She wrote continuously, tossing the pages on the floor as she filled them, until late morning. Then she would rise, bathe and dress for lunch, sometimes taking time for a stroll in the garden, where she gave orders to the gardeners. Meanwhile, her maid gathered up the myriad pages from the floor and took them to the secretary (who lived at The Mount when the Whartons were in residence) to be typed and readied for the next day's revisions.

The rest of the day would then be devoted to rides through the countryside, letter writing and reading, ending with a quiet dinner in the evening. She realized that this schedule was not always to the liking of her old friends. In one letter written during her early days at The Mount, she acknowledged this, saying, "I seldom ask people to stay because I am obliged to lead such a quiet and systematic kind of life that the house is a dull one for visitors."

The Mount reflects Edith Wharton's enthusiasm for classical design.

The house, though quite large, was purposely designed for entertaining on a small scale. She had left Newport to escape the daily round of social activities and did not want to duplicate that scene in her quiet Berkshire retreat. The entrance to the house itself is off to one side (actually considered the back of the house) where the door leads to a small enclosed hall. Upon entering the hall, the visitor gets no hint of the spacious rooms in the front of the house that look out over formal gardens, Laurel Lake and the beautiful Berkshire Mountains beyond.

Many of Wharton's major works were written while she lived at The Mount, including *The Valley of Decision, The House of Mirth* and one of her most celebrated novels, *Ethan Frome.* The last is the tragic love

---

The Little Red House

In the mid-1800s, long before Edith Wharton built her home in the Berkshires, the area had been a refuge for such writers as Catherine Sedgwick, Herman Melville, William Cullen Bryant, Oliver Wendell Holmes and—perhaps the most famous—Nathanial Hawthorne.

Nathanial and Sophie Hawthorne rented a small red cottage in Stockbridge just as Hawthorne completed writing *The Scarlet Letter.* When Sophie described their new home as "The Little Red Shanty," Nathanial remarked that it was "as red as a scarlet letter."

While living there, Hawthorne wrote *The House of the Seven Gables, The Wonder Book* and *Tanglewood Tales.* His benefactors, the Tappans, were living temporarily at Highwood, the estate on which The Little Red House was located. Tappan later built his own estate on nearby property, naming it Tanglewood after Hawthorne's book. In the 1930s, the Tappans' granddaughter made a gift of the property to the Berkshire Musical Festival, now the summer home of the renowned Boston Symphony Orchestra.

The red cottage burned to the ground in the 1890s, but was completely reconstructed in 1947 on the original foundation. It contains period furniture and first editions of Hawthorne's works. It is used for practice rooms for music students; during July and August tours are conducted. For information call 413-637-1666.

story of a poor Berkshire farmer, and Wharton chose Lenox as the setting. Tourists often roam through the town looking for some of the sights depicted in the book, particularly the hill where the dramatic sledding accident was supposed to have occurred.

In 1920 Wharton was awarded the Pulitzer Prize for *The Age of Innocence*, the first woman novelist to receive this prestigious award. She was not happy about winning it, however, as the judges saw the book—which she wrote as an indictment of New York society—as "the highest standard of American manners and manhood." In writing to Sinclair Lewis, whom she felt should have won the prize, she said, "When I discovered that I was being rewarded—by one of our leading Universities (Columbia)—for uplifting American morals, I confess, I *did* despair."

For the past several years The Mount, now a National Historic Landmark, has been undergoing extensive restoration. Edith Wharton matinee plays are performed on summer afternoons by Shakespeare and Company. Other fund-raising activities, including house and garden tours, are given throughout the summer months. The tours focus on the literary, historical and biographical details of Wharton's life and writings.

Today, artists still set up their easels on the lawn of the Florence Griswold Museum.

Artists' Haunts

The mountains and shores of New England provide artists with a never-ending supply of visual ideas. Painters, potters and other craftspeople flock to the region simply to capture its natural beauty in their work.

Small artists' colonies have flourished up and down the coast, along the rivers and into the mountains of New England. Two of the best-known among these are located in Old Lyme, Connecticut, and Rockport, Massachusetts. The small enclave started by "Miss Florence" in Old Lyme is now open to the public as the Florence Griswold Museum. It became America's best-known center of Impressionist painting at the turn of the century. Rockport, Massachusetts, is said to have been home to nearly all the leading names in American art, evidenced by the frequently painted scene of fishing shacks and lobster pots.

Artists from John Singleton Copley to Andrew Wyeth have found inspiration in the New England scene. Here are their stories.

The Most Famous Corkscrew in America

Codman Road
Lincoln, Mass.
617-259-8843

OPEN:
June 1–October 15
Wed–Sun: 12–5

ADMISSION:
Inquire for prices.

The Grange/Codman House

Lincoln, Massachusetts
1 7 4 1

During the late eighteenth century, the room just off the left side of the front hallway in The Grange was used as a small dining chamber. It was in this room that, one fine autumn evening, Dr. Charles Russell was entertaining the American portrait painter John Singleton Copley. Dr. Russell had commissioned Copley to paint his portrait, and the artist had traveled the 15 miles to Lincoln from Boston by carriage, bringing his paints with him.

Just before dinner, Russell excused himself for a moment to go down to the wine cellar to fetch a bottle of wine that he was saving for the occasion. After retrieving it, however, he discovered his corkscrew was missing. He searched the house in vain, but to no avail. Dr. Russell was distraught. He prided himself on being an excellent host and it would not do to be unable to serve his guest a good wine with dinner. His only recourse was to borrow one from his next-door neighbor. Unfortunately, his nearest neighbor lived over ten miles away. Undaunted, Dr. Russell quickly saddled his horse and rode off to get the corkscrew. Winded and out of breath, he returned in reasonably good time with the borrowed corkscrew, opened the wine, and he and Copley enjoyed a most satisfactory meal.

After both gentlemen retired for the evening, Copley silently returned to the dining chamber. With his oils and brushes in hand, he painted a wonderful corkscrew on the door to the wine cellar. Copley, known for his wit and charm, explained the painting to his surprised host the next morning by saying, "Allow me, sir, to see to it that your house is never again without a corkscrew."

Today, this painting is now the proud possession of

the Museum of Fine Arts in Boston. It is highly prized for three reasons: It is the first American *trompe l'oeil;* it is the earliest known American still life; and it is the only still life ever done by John Singleton Copley.

This stately house contains the first American *trompe l'oeil* painting.

An interesting aside to this story is the fate of the portrait of Charles Russell, which was thought missing for many years. Badly damaged, it was given to the Massachusetts Historical Society in 1952 by Miss Mary Curtiss, a relative who had inherited it. She explained the mutilation of the portrait: One of the daughters of Dr. Russell, "feeling wronged that her sister had inherited the painting, slashed out the head in a fit of jealousy, folded it up and carried it in her dress pocket all her life."

The Grange, an elegant Federal-syle mansion, is also known as The Codman House. Dr. Russell's youngest sister, Margaret, who inherited the property, was married to John Codman. It was used as a summer residence by the Codman family for over 200 years, until it was bequeathed to the Society for the Preservation of New England Antiquities in 1968. It is filled with the family's collections, furnishings and personal belongings, reflecting their cultured nineteenth-century lifestyle.

Opposites Attract

No two museum houses could be more different than the Codman House and the Gropius House, yet they both share the same country neighborhood in Lincoln, Massachusetts. In marked contrast to the eighteenth-century Georgian architecture and cluttered Victorian interior of the Codman House, the Gropius House expresses, inside and out, the twentieth-century Bauhaus principles of function and simplicity.

Walter Gropius is recognized today as one of the most innovative and influential architects of the twentieth century. He was the Director of the Bauhaus (school of design) in Germany from 1919 through 1928. When he came to teach at Harvard's Graduate School of Design in 1937, he built this thoroughly modern, innovative house for his family. It is a combination of native New England building materials—wood, brick and fieldstone—and the latest in modern technology—glass block, chrome and acoustical plaster.

The house has been preserved with its original furnishings by the Society for the Preservation of New England Antiquities. The house contains furniture made expressly for it in the Bauhaus workshop in Germany, as well as works of art and other personal belongings of the Gropius family. It is open on certain weekends throughout the year. For information call 617-259-8843.

The Impressionists of Old Lyme

The Florence Griswold Museum

Old Lyme, Connecticut

1817

96 Lyme Street
Old Lyme, Conn.
203-434-5542

OPEN:
June–October
Tues–Sat: 10–5
Sun: 1–5

November–May
Wed–Sun: 1–5

ADMISSION:
Inquire for prices.

As the last surviving member of her family, Florence Griswold was determined to hold on to the family homestead, a beautiful late-Georgian house with four massive columns across its facade enclosing a grand portico. Her father had been a prosperous sea captain, but upon his death in 1882, she and her mother were forced to turn the house into a finishing school to pay their debts.

When her mother died, Florence, keenly interested in the arts, decided to transform the house and grounds into an artists' retreat. Its setting in the lovely coastal town of Old Lyme, Connecticut, attracted many of the turn-of-the-century landscape artists who were just beginning to experiment with and be influenced by the French Barbizon and Impressionist styles of painting.

The Griswold House soon became well known as an artists' colony where such "boarders" as Childe Hassam, Willard Metcalf, Walter Griffin and Henry Ranger came for the summer to paint. "Miss Florence," as they called her, turned the large front hallway into a gallery where their paintings were sold. She also arranged for an exhibit for her "boys" at the local library each summer where their paintings were eagerly snapped up by local collectors.

Not all the painters who came to the colony were well established. Many of them were unable to pay for their room and board. But thanks to the generosity and trust of their host, Miss Florence, they never feared for their survival. The best example of her faith in her students is told in a story written down by the distinguished Canadian painter Arthur Heming, who spent many happy summers in Old Lyme.

At the annual art exhibition one summer, none of

Willard Metcalf's paintings had sold. Worried and embarrassed that he could not pay his rent, he spent the next several days painting a picture of the Griswold house. He showed the house bathed in moonlight with Miss Florence in the foreground walking up a stone path, and he called it "May Night."

When he presented it to Miss Florence to pay off the debt he owed her, she was thrilled. But she refused to keep the painting, insisting instead that he show it in New York. This was the turning point in Metcalf's career, according to Heming. When the painting was shown the following winter at the prestigious Corcoran Art Gallery in Washington, it not only won the Clark Gold Medal but was purchased by the gallery for its permanent collection. His success soared from that time on and, according to Heming, "Metcalf died a wealthy man."

In 1968, when Miss Florence became unable to care for the house, her many friends and relatives formed the Florence Griswold Association to care for her and to turn the house into a museum of history and art. Today, it is a thriving art museum with over 900

The Florence Griswold Museum displays the artwork of over 100 American artists.

works of art by 130 American artists. Thousands of
visitors tour the museum each year. What many come
to see are the murals painted by some of the early Impressionists. Landscapes, trees and flowers adorn the
doors and walls, and across the mantle in the dining
room the artists painted a caricature of themselves
called "The Fox Hunt."

More Sights in Old Lyme

The Florence Griswold Museum stands in Old Lyme, one of the
most elegant little seafaring towns in New England. Its quiet, tree-
shaded main street, now a historic district, is lined with a number of
graceful old homes built in the 1700s by wealthy sea captains. The
later influence of the early American Impressionist artists who came
to live and work here has left a lasting imprint as well.

On most sunny days, artists sit at their easels under the shade
trees on Lyme Street or down by the edge of the Lieutenant River
capturing the landscape on canvas. Galleries and studios abound,
and the works of local artists are constantly on display. The more
prominent galleries are the Lyme Academy of Fine Arts (84 Lyme
Street) and those at the Lyme Art Association (Lyme Street at Route
1). The latter, founded in 1902, it is the oldest summer art group in
the country.

Recently, the studio once used by artist William Chadwick was
moved to the grounds of the Florence Griswold Museum. Chadwick
was among the group of early American Impressionist painters who
made their home in Old Lyme. His rural landscape paintings of Old
Lyme hang in many prominent art galleries. Chadwick's studio has
been fully restored with all of its original furnishings and is open to
visitors.

There are two particularly nice inns for lunch, dinner or overnight
accommodations if you are planning a stay in Old Lyme. Try the Old
Lyme Inn (85 Lyme Street, 203-434-5352) and the Bee & Thistle Inn
(100 Lyme Street, 203-434-1667).

Mrs. Jack

280 The Fenway
Boston, Mass.
617-566-1401

OPEN:
July–August
Tues–Sun: 12–5
September–June
Tues: 12–6:30
Wed–Sun: 12–5

ADMISSION:
Inquire for prices.

Fenway Court

Boston, Massachusetts
1903

Isabella Stewart Gardner was one of the most exciting and colorful women to brighten the somber Victorian scene in Boston during the mid-nineteenth century. Born in New York and educated abroad, she moved to Boston in 1860 when she married one of the town's wealthiest and most eligible bachelors, John Lowell Gardner.

Like many newcomers to Boston society before her, Isabella was snubbed as an outsider by the proper Boston Brahmins. A brilliant and spirited young woman, she retaliated by becoming just about as improper and outrageous as she could.

Her antics soon became legend. She walked down Tremont Street with a lion named Rex on a leash. On shopping trips around Boston she never left her carriage, insisting that salesmen accommodate her with curb service. Instead of drinking tea she drank beer. She poked fun at the many exclusive Boston clubs by forming her own and calling it the "It" club. While other Boston women kept their jewels locked away, she wore two huge diamonds set on gold wire springs so they fluttered above her head like butterfly antennae. She greeted guests to her Beacon Street home from the bottom branch of a mimosa tree.

John Singer Sargent painted her portrait, and even that created a scandal. She posed in a black low-necked gown with a rope of pearls around her waist and a black shawl drawn about her hips to accentuate her figure. When the portrait was exhibited, it generated so many hostile comments that Mr. Gardner declared he would never exhibit it again.

"Mrs. Jack," as she was often called by intimates, became, through the years, a connoisseur of fine art and antiques and acquired a large collection during her many travels abroad. When her husband died, she decided to build a palace to house her treasures. She constructed a magnificent Venetian *palazzo*, and kept it hidden from the public by a tall fence until it was finished.

The grand opening of her new home, Fenway Court, was held on a cold, wintry New Year's Day in 1903. The dazzled guests were greeted by music—the Boston Symphony Orchestra. Cascading masses of fragrant flowers and flickering candles decorated the multitiered balconies, and a flower-bedecked, glistening fountain graced the center of a large indoor courtyard.

Isabella Stewart Gardner, as painted by J. S. Sargent.

Today, visiting Fenway Court, you will enjoy seeing the Italian architecture with Chinese and Spanish influences in many of the rooms. A rich collection of paintings by Raphael, Rembrandt and Rubens, as well as such nineteenth-century artists as Sargent, Manet, Degas and Whistler is on display. And, of course, so is the famous portrait of "Mrs. Jack," by Sargent.

As stated in Isabella's will, everything has been kept exactly as she left it, including the cascades of fragrant flowers surrounding the central courtyard with its splashing fountain.

Isabella's Competition

The Museum of Fine Arts is in the same neighborhood and only a short walk from the Gardner Museum. "Mrs. Jack" carried on a celebrated rivalry with the museum, not only in acquisitions, but in rushing to complete Fenway Court before the new fine arts building was even begun.

While the Gardner has remained a small gem of a museum (as specified by Isabella's will), the Museum of Fine Arts has continued to expand and grow. It now ranks among the most important art museums in the world, second only to the New York "Met" for its comprehensive collections. Exhibits include a wide range of periods—from ancient Minoan civilization artifacts to twentieth-century paintings. All the important schools of European art are represented here, including a fine collection of French Impressionists and the Old Masters.

Of exceptional quality are the American decorative arts and sculpture and the American period rooms with displays of eighteenth- and nineteenth-century furnishings. The 1981 west wing addition hosts major traveling exhibits.

The museum, located at 465 Huntington Avenue, is open every day except Monday. The new wing houses a café and gourmet dining. Call 617-267-9300.

Christina's World

The Olson Homestead
Cushing, Maine
1801

Hathorn Point Road
Cushing, Maine
207-596-6457

OPEN:
June–September
Wed–Sun: 11–4

ADMISSION:
Inquire for prices.
Note: Please park
and walk in
designated areas
only.

One of the most instantly recognizable modern American paintings—and one that never fails to evoke an emotional response from the viewer—is Andrew Wyeth's "Christina's World." It is a painting of Christina Olson, a friend and neighbor of Wyeth's during his long summer stays in Cushing, Maine.

In the fall of 1892, an early freeze on the St. George River forced a young Swedish sailor, John Olson, ashore and he sought refuge in the Hathorn farmhouse. There he met the Hathorn's daughter Kate, married her soon after and gave up the sea for farming. They had four children: Christina, born in 1893; Alvaro, born the next year; and Samuel and Fred, who followed soon after.

When Christina was 3½ years old, she became ill and developed a severe limp. Polio, its effects and its treatment were unknown in those days, and Christina's lameness was taken for granted. Along with the other children in the family, she walked the 1½ miles to school every day, where she was said to be an extremely bright and attentive student.

After their parents died, Sam and Fred Olson married and bought their own farms. Christina and Alvaro stayed on at the old homestead, working the farm and looking out for one another. As the years progressed, however, the crippling effects of polio began to take their toll on Christina. When she could no longer walk, she crawled about using her arms. It was in this position that Wyeth painted her, as she was making her way across the wide, grassy field toward the house. Although she was 55 years old at the time, Wyeth painted her as a much younger woman, visually capturing on canvas the struggle and constraints of her life.

Christina and Alvaro died just weeks apart in 1968. Upon hearing the news, Wyeth visited the farm one more time to paint his last picture of his dear friends. This time his painting was symbolic rather than a true portrait. A watercolor entitled "Alvaro and Christina" shows a shadowy black door for Alvaro and a bright blue one for Christina. Old pots and pans, a peach basket and a few farm implements are nearby, and hanging on a nail by the blue door is a crumpled pink rag, a remnant of a dress once worn by Christina.

Soon after their deaths, the house was put up for sale and its furnishings were auctioned off. It was purchased by film producer Joseph E. Levine who, as a tribute to Wyeth, completely restored the house and opened it to the public. At that time, however, the neighbors greatly resented the intrusion of so many tourists to their usually quiet neighborhood. This created considerable negative publicity and because of it, Levine closed and sold the house.

The house was then sold to John Sculley, the former president of Apple Computers, and his wife, Lee. The Sculleys put the house and its surrounding 20 acres on the market in 1989 for $1.25 million. With no serious buyer in sight, they decided to donate the house

The Olson Homestead, home of Christina, who was made famous by Andrew Wyeth.

and two acres of land to the Farnsworth Art Museum in nearby Rockland.

The museum has had a strong connection with the Wyeth family over the years with paintings by all three generations—N. C., Andrew, and Jamie—well represented there. It is particularly appropriate that this museum, considered one of the finest regional art museums in the nation, should be the guardian of a house that, according to Andrew Wyeth, held "the whole history of New England."

Inspiration Island

Artist Jamie Wyeth (son of Andrew) has found his source of inspiration on Monhegan Island, nine miles off the coast of Maine. Monhegan has been a haven for artists since Rockwell Kent began coming here with his friends in the early 1900s. (Wyeth now lives in Kent's former home.) Word spread, and now Monhegan Island is home to more artists than lobstermen during the summer—and lobstering is Monhegan's main industry.

This is a rugged little island, only about 1½ miles in length and barely 1 mile wide. Less than 100 people live here year-round—those who don't miss telephones, televisions or microwaves. Electricity is scarce here, and kerosene lamps and candles are used not for effect but out of necessity.

In the summer, the population triples. Anxious vacationers come to Monhegan to get away from it all—and Monhegan is definitely the place to do just that. The small village—a cluster of weathered cottages, fishing shacks and a few food and gift shops—overlooks the harbor. Dominating the village is the Island Inn, a large, rambling building where day-trippers can stop for lunch. While other places on the island offer lodgings, the Island Inn is the only one that is fully electrified.

Hiking along the island's trails, bird-watching, swimming and visiting artists' studios (a schedule is posted each day) are among the favored activities here. To get to this out-of-the-way spot, day-trippers can take the *Balmy Days* out of Boothbay Harbor (207-633-2284) or, for longer visits (there are several bed-and-breakfasts on the island), take the *Laura B* out of Port Clyde (207-372-8848).

The Musical Wonder House, where each room greets visitors with a new melody.

Funhouses

Some of New England's open houses are just plain fun to visit. These are not houses of great historical interest or architectural distinction, but ones that provide the backdrop for a unique experience for visitors.

What could be more fun then visiting a house made completely out of paper—inside and out? Or a house where music fills the air and each room has an amazing musical discovery? There's a house in the woods where the "big bad wolf" still sleeps—but he's no threat to those who come to dine on food cooked with delicious home-grown herbs. At one house on Cape Cod you can watch fresh jam being cooked by the sun and take a stroll along the paths where storybook animals seem to come to life. And there's a house you can visit in Connecticut that can offer you a view unrivaled by any other in New England. These houses are particularly fun to visit with children—but no less fun for adults.

6 Discovery Road
East Sandwich,
Mass.
617-888-6870

OPEN:
May–December
Mon–Sat: 10–4
Sun: 1–4

ADMISSION:
Free.

Green Briar Nature Center

East Sandwich, Massachusetts

1 7 5 6

If I should walk in Gully Lane
Think you that I would find
The boyhood lost so long ago
The youth I left behind?

These first few lines of a sentimental little poem written many years ago by Thornton W. Burgess—beloved Cape Cod author of 170 books and more than 15,000 newspaper stories—probably best describe that whimsical, nostalgic pull that lures thousands of young and old visitors each summer not only to Gully Lane, but to Smiling Pool, Laughing Brook, the Crooked Little Path, the Green Meadows and, of course, The Old Briar Patch—which can all be found at the Green Briar Nature Center.

Burgess was born in Sandwich in 1874, later moving to Springfield, where he became an editor for a local publishing company. In the early 1900s, he began writing bedtime stories for his young son, based on his childhood memories of the woods he had roamed as a boy in Sandwich. Perhaps inspired by the tales of fictional rabbits that were beginning to appear in abundance at that time (Beatrix Potter's *The Tale of Peter Rabbit,* Joel Chandler Harris's *Br'er Rabbit* and Howard Garis's *Uncle Wiggly*), Burgess centered his tales on a group of friendly animals that inhabited the briar patch—Hooty the Owl, Jerry Muskrat, Mrs. Possum, Jimmy Skunk and, of course, Peter Cottontail. Their stories were compiled into such books as *Bedtime Stories, Old Mother West Wind* and *The Adventures of Peter Cottontail.*

What set Burgess apart from the other children's story writers of his day was his love of nature and his concern for the natural environment of his animals. A

Characters from the stories of Thornton Burgess decorate his commemorative plaque and the natural landscape preserved in his honor.

conservationist and naturalist by nature rather than by formal education, he has been credited (and honored) by many conservation societies, naturalists and individuals with developing in his young readers a love of nature and a sense of social and moral responsibility toward living things.

A short walk around the pond or along the crooked path at the Green Briar Nature Center will make you think that time has indeed stood still. You half expect Peter Cottontail and one of his friends—Happy Jack, Reddy Fox or Johnny Chuck—to scurry out of the underbrush. The nature center is now several acres of conservation land owned and operated by The Thornton W. Burgess Society of Sandwich, Massachusetts. Throughout the year, nature classes, walks, lectures and other programs are held here—the same locale that provided the background for Burgess' famous children's stories.

Would clutching hands of bramble bush
Still reach to hold me fast
or would they treat me as a ghost
A vision of the past?

The bramble bushes still grow wild here, but the well-worn path keeps their "clutching hands" from snagging on clothes as you walk the historic old Briar Patch Trail. This mile-long, self-guided adventure takes you through thickets of bull briar, stands of tall oaks, maples and pines, delicious-tasting highbush blueberry and fragrant swamp honeysuckle.

In 1974, on the 100th anniversary of his birth, a museum was established in Burgess' name in the center of historic Sandwich (in the 1756 Deacon Eldred House) which now contains a large collection of Burgess memorabilia. It is only a short distance away from the Green Briar Nature Center (which also includes The Green Briar Jam Kitchen).

When Burgess was a boy, his neighbor, Ida Putnam, had a very successful jam business here, and Burgess often dropped by to sample her wares. Today, the kitchen of Ida's house is much as it was in her day, and her delicious "sun-cooked" jam is still made and sold here. Over the door of the kitchen is a plaque with an inscription that Burgess had written on one of his books he sent to her, "It's a wonderful thing to sweeten the world which is in a jam and needs preserving."

Returning to the little poem we started with, Burgess concluded it with these lines:

Ah me! So many years have fled
and mingled joy with pain
I fear to seek the boy who once
Did walk in Gully Lane.

Chances are, were he alive today, Burgess would have little trouble discovering the delights of that small boy of long ago on a return visit to the Old Briar Patch.

Historic Sandwich

Sandwich, the birthplace of Thornton W. Burgess, is the oldest town on Cape Cod. In 1637 Plymouth Colony granted to "Ten Men from Saugus" the right to settle enough land "for three score families." Three seventeenth-century houses have survived (two are in what is now East Sandwich) and are open to the public in the summer: The Wing Fort House (508-888-3591), The Nye Homestead (508-888-4213) and the Old Hoxie House (508-888-0251). The Thomas Dexter Grist Mill (508-888-1173), in the center of the village by the Mill Pond, was completely restored in 1961—and it grinds corn daily from mid-June to early October.

Also in Sandwich is the Thornton Burgess Museum (508-888-4668). The museum contains the largest known collection of Thornton Burgess writings, original Harrison Cady illustrations and natural history exhibits relating to the life and work of Thornton Burgess. There is also an excellent book and gift shop here where "Story Time" is held two afternoons a week during the summer.

The most important industry in Sandwich was that of glassmaking, and the glass made here in the nineteenth century became world famous. The Sandwich Glass Museum displays the renowned collection here and gives tours year-round. Call 508-888-0251 for information.

Heritage Plantation, not far from the village of Sandwich, has one of the finest rhododendron displays in the country. This 76-acre site is the former estate of champion rhododendron breeder Charles O. Dexter. Visitors can see thousands of plants from May to July. An authentic reproduction of a Shaker barn houses a collection of vintage cars; another building displays exhibits of Americana—early tools, miniature soldiers, firearms and much more. A motorized bus takes visitors around the plantation and there is a café and a picnic area for lunch. Call 508-888-3300 for information on the Heritage Plantation.

Recycling at Its Best

Pigeon Hill Street
Rockport, Mass.
508-546-2629

OPEN:
July–August
Daily: 10–5
Call for spring and
fall hours.

ADMISSION:
Inquire for prices.

Paper House

Rockport, Massachusetts
1 9 2 2

When it comes to recycling, the Stenman family of Pigeon Cove, Massachusetts, was way ahead of the times. Mr. Elis F. Stenman, a Swedish immigrant, read a half-dozen newspapers each day—local, national and foreign. He saved them all and put them to good use when he built his amazing summer house. This building is a one-floor dwelling with a low pitched roof; a long front porch stretches across the front. On first glance, it looks like an ordinary summer cottage. On closer inspection you will see that the entire house (except for the brick chimney) is made of paper.

Mr. Stenman and his family created the house, complete with paper furniture, from approximately 100,000 newspapers. The experiment, begun in 1922, was to see what could be done with newspapers without destroying the print. Sheets of newspaper were folded into layers and carefully pasted so that the print would not be blurred. This produced a finished product that was both strong and stable and could be used as a building material. And what an interesting material it is—you can actually read the furniture!

Tables, chairs, lamps and a settee shaped like octagons consist of Boston newspapers, including some early copies of the *Christian Science Monitor*. A writing desk (nicknamed "The Lindberg Desk") is made from copies of newspapers reporting Colonel Charles Lindberg's flight. A 1928 radio cabinet is covered with news of Hoover's campaign for president. A large grandfather clock is made of newspapers from all the capital cities of the then 48 states, and the title of each paper is clearly visible. The fireplace mantel and hood, extending to the ceiling, are constructed of the rotogravure section of the *Boston Sunday Herald* and the *New York Tribune*.

The exterior walls of the house consist of 215 thicknesses of paper pressed under two tons of pressure, as were the shingles for the roof. The entire project took 20 years of steady work to complete. While it is a cozy, livable cottage (you could sleep fairly comfortably on the cot made from newspapers reporting on World War I), it is now kept as a special exhibit house, open to visitors who frequent this scenic area of Cape Ann.

A Grandfather clock in the Paper House.

The Other Cape

Rockport, located on the tip of Cape Ann (the "other cape" of Massachusetts) has one of the most picturesque harbors along the New England coast. It is still an active fishing village but has become world-famous as a gathering spot for artists. "Motif #1" at the end of Tuna Wharf is said to be "the world's most painted and photographed lobster shack."

The narrow, winding streets of Rockport are crowded with art galleries, shops and eating places. Bearskin Neck, a rocky peninsula of land off Dock Square on Main Street, is the epitome of quaintness. Once the commercial center of town, the old weather-beaten shacks where lobstermen and fishermen stored their gear are now filled with such things as souvenirs, gifts, T-shirts, penny candy, jewelry and arts and crafts shops.

Rockport is a "dry" town, thanks to Hannah Jumper. Hannah was the leader of the "Hatchet Gang." On July 8, 1856, Hannah led 200 angry, hatchet-wielding housewives on a destructive rampage. For five hours they and their supporters sought out the shops where they suspected liquor was being sold to their husbands and friends. Kegs, jugs and casks were rolled out into the street and quickly smashed to bits. The goal of these woman was to destroy "for all time" sales of liquor in Rockport—and they succeeded!

The Sound of Music

Musical Wonder House
Wiscasset, Maine
1852

18 High Street
Wiscasset, Maine
207-882-7163

OPEN:
Memorial Day–
October 15
Daily: 10–5

ADMISSION:
Inquire for prices.

Stepping inside the Musical Wonder House is like stepping into a Victorian music box. The front door triggers a signal as you enter, and you are immediately surrounded by the old familiar tinkling strains of a Viennese waltz or a Mozart sonata. As you look about for more wonderous happenings, you will find the inevitable dancing ballerina.

Every room in this house is filled with what is considered the most extensive collection of music boxes (or mechanical musical instruments) in the country; many of them are one of a kind. Smaller pieces include small musical beer steins from Germany and Switzerland that play a single melody. A more elaborate music box is an oversize orchestral version that plays a program of 72 compositions.

There are many fascinating wonders in this house, such as a Dutch organ clock made in 1780 and a rare Grand Format Cylinder Musical Box made in Switzerland in 1855 that plays an operatic program of 24 arias. The oldest piece, a French miniature pipe organ, dates from 1740. One particularly delightful piece is a colorful candy-dispensing Swiss orchestral music box. It features a snare drum, orchestral bells, castanets, two butterfly bell strikers, two Chinese figures operating four bells and six bisque dolls dancing to the music. When the music stops playing, a handful of candy mints drop down.

The backdrop for this wonderful collection is a fully restored 1852 sea captain's house built by two brothers. Many of the original classic details remain, such as a handsome flying staircase in the front entrance hall. The rooms are furnished with period antiques and arranged to display the collection of musical instruments.

Danilo Konvalinka, seated at a 1912 A. B. Chase Artisano player piano.

The Musical Wonder House is now the home of Mr. and Mrs. Danilo Konvalinka. As a young man growing up in Austria, Danilo became fascinated with music boxes. Soon after coming to America, he purchased his first one. He learned to repair them and set up his own shop in Washington, D.C. On a vacation trip to Maine in the 1960s, he and his wife discovered the old captain's house for sale. It was just what they were looking for to restore and turn into a museum to house their growing music box collection.

Danilo now has a studio here for restoring and repairing music boxes, and has opened his home to the public for guided tours and demonstrations. He leads most of the tours himself, which often includes his playing a piece on a rare 1912 A. B. Chase player piano. During the summer months there are also candlelight concerts at the house.

If you want to take a bit of the nostalgic music home with you, the well-stocked gift shop offers duplicate instruments for sale, as well as an assortment of small music boxes from Switzerland and Japan.

Castle Tucker

On the top of Windmill Hill in Wiscasset, Maine, a fascinating house with enormous windows commands a panoramic view of the town and harbor. It has become known locally as Castle Tucker, and was originally built in 1807 by Judge Silas Lee, a Wiscasset lawyer, who supposedly patterned it after a castle in Dunbar, Scotland. (Researchers have found no such castle in Scotland.)

The brick walls of the castle rise three stories high, ending with a widow's walk on the slightly pitched roof. Rounded side wings balloon out on both sides of the house and a glass facade of triple windows on the east side faces the harbor.

One of the many rumors that surrounds Castle Tucker is that Lee never paid his architect and, in turn, the architect laid a curse on the castle: "Whoever lives here must come to poverty." When Lee died in 1814, he left the house—heavily mortgaged—to three of his neighbors.

For 23 years Castle Tucker was alternately rented to a series of tenants and left vacant. Strange tales and wild rumors soon gave it a reputation for being a haunted house. It was eventually purchased by Captain Richard H. Tucker, Jr., a third-generation Wiscasset ship captain and owner. He and his new bride made several changes in the house and filled it with Victorian antiques. His daughter still lives in the house with all its original furnishings, and welcomes visitors during July and August and other times by appointment. Call 207-882-7364 for details.

Grandmother's House

Nutting Hill Road
Mason, N.H.
603-878-1151

OPEN:
Year-round
Daily: 10–5

ADMISSION:
Free to cottage and
grounds.
Note: Reservations
are required for
lunch. Seatings at
11:30, 12:45, and 2.

Pickity Place

Mason, New Hampshire
1 7 8 0

The storybook house of *Little Red Riding Hood* comes to life in a clearing in the woods outside the little village of Mason, New Hampshire. The small cottage is just as you may have remembered it from your bedtime-story days: a dark-shingled, Cape-style dwelling with tidy shutters and neatly trimmed hedges, half-hidden behind an enormous old gnarled ash tree, surrounded by old-fashioned flower and herb gardens.

Neither Grandmother nor Little Red Riding Hood are anywhere in sight, but if you step through the front door of Pickity Place and peek through the bedroom doorway, you'll find the big, bad wolf (stuffed, of course) all snuggled down, nightcap and all, in Grandma's big bed.

Pickity Place is the current name for the house that was the setting for the 1948 Golden Book version of the classic story illustrated by Elizabeth Orton Jones. In the mid-1940s, Jones, an illustrator, had recently come to Mason to show author Gladys Adshead some illustrations she had just completed for Adshead's latest book. She fell in love with the little house that stood next door to Adshead's and, when she heard it was for sale for back taxes—and for the same amount as a royalty check she had just received—she bought it without hesitation.

Later, when she was asked by Golden Books to adapt *Little Red Riding Hood* for them, she was delighted. She knew right away she had not only the perfect house for her model of Grandmother's house, but the woods surrounding it, as well, to complete the scene.

The winding dirt road up to the 200-year-old house is over a mile long, with many ruts and bumps—an

adventure in itself. But thankfully, no wolves seem to cross this path. The house has now been completely restored and turned into a wonderful gourmet restaurant and herbarium. One room in the house, a first-floor bedroom, has been restored to duplicate exactly Jones's illustration of Grandmother's bedroom. (This is where the wolf permanently resides!)

The storybook Pickity Place, home to Little Red Riding Hood's grandmother.

Current owners Judy and David Walter began growing herbs 20 years ago, first as a hobby. Their "hobby" has now mushroomed into an internationally known herb business. Their small restaurant in the original dining room of the house is so popular that reservations are taken months in advance. While parents dine on gourmet fare flavored with fresh herbs from the garden, children are served with a picnic basket filled with foods more suited to their tastes (peanut butter and jelly sandwiches, cheesburgers and pizza).

Fresh herbs and plants are sold in both the gift shop and greenhouses, and flower gardens abound.

Red Riding Hood would have loved this place!

Barrett House

The tiny hamlet of New Ipswich, New Hampshire is just a short drive from Mason, and it is surprising to find such an imposing three-story Federal-style mansion as Barrett House (the antithesis of Pickity Place) in these country surroundings. Legend has it that when Charles Barrett, Jr., was about to be married, his father-in-law-to-be, Jonas Minot, challenged Charles Barrett, Sr., to a wager: If the senior Barrett would build the young couple a grand house, Minot would furnish it in grand style. And so they did.

Charles Barrett, Sr., was already a wealthy man when he entered into a partnership that financed one of New England's earliest textile mills. It was built on the Souhegan River in New Ipswich and brought prosperity to the small town in the early 1800s. With the eventual closing of the mills, the town retreated to its quiet, rural ways.

The house remained in the Barrett family as a summer residence from the late nineteenth century until 1948. It was then donated, along with all the furnishings, to the Society for the Preservation of New England Antiquities. This accounts for its excellent condition and faithful interpretation of the elegance and leisurely lifestyle enjoyed by the nineteenth-century gentry.

In 1979, the Barrett House was further recognized for its authenticity when it was chosen by filmmakers as the perfect setting for "The Europeans" (based on the Henry James classical novel about two expatriates and their sober American relatives). Call 617-227-3956 for information.

Bavaria in Connecticut

Heublein Tower

Simsbury, Connecticut

1914

Talcott Mountain
State Park
Route 185
Simsbury, Conn.
203-566-2304
203-677-0662

OPEN:
April–Memorial Day
Weekends: 10–5
June 1-Labor Day
Daily: 10–5
Labor Day–
November 1
Weekends: 10–5
The park and trails
are open year-round.

ADMISSION:
Free.

Soaring high above the treetops on Talcott Mountain in the town of Simsbury, Connecticut, stands the historic Heublein Tower. Located just seven miles west of Hartford, it has been a familiar landmark in this area for the past 80 years. In the observation room at the top of the 165-foot tower, visitors are treated to a magnificent 360-degree view of the central portion of the state. On a clear day, the view extends beyond the state's borders to Long Island Sound to the south and the distant mountains of northern New England to the north.

This unique structure, sturdily built with a steel frame and reinforced concrete, was designed by Gilbert F. Heublein "to never blow over." Heublein, a well-known hotelier and restaurateur in Hartford, was born in Suhl, Bavaria, in 1849. He and his family, a part of the large exodus during the Prussian Revolution, immigrated to this country a year later. They settled in Beacon Falls, Connecticut, not far from the city of New Haven.

Albert Heublein, Gilbert's father, earned a living as a weaver until he could afford to open a restaurant—specializing in German food—on the green in New Haven. This was the beginning of a very successful family enterprise. The family later moved to the Hartford area, opened a second restaurant, and eventually started a business of importing and exporting such gourmet delicacies as rare wines, liquors, bay rum and olive oil.

Gilbert joined his father's business as a salesman at the age of 18 and three years later was made a full partner. The business was then named "Andrew Heublein and Son." When Gilbert's younger brother Louis joined the firm, their father retired and it became known as "G. F. Heublein and Brother."

Gilbert was instrumental in introducing many specialities under the family brand name, particularly packaged and bottled cocktail mixes and a popular condiment, now known as A.1. Sauce. In addition, they ventured into hotels—in 1891, the brothers opened the Heublein Hotel in Hartford, which was considered the finest in New England and earned a nationwide reputation for its food and comfort. Carpeted with Oriental rugs and decorated with fine furnishings, it boasted of "a window in every room." The dining room, however, was its outstanding feature, quickly becoming known for its excellent gourmet food. Many notables were among the guests

From the Heublein Tower visitors are treated to an incomparable view.

at the hotel, and it was a particular favorite of theatrical companies that stopped there.

Gilbert Heublein was an active sportsman (his hotel was always filled during the hunting and fishing season) and an avid automobile racer. He loved to travel and took many trips to his native Bavaria. He became fascinated with the distinctive and numerous towers of the small village of Dinklesbuhl close to his birthplace and, upon his return from one of his many visits, decided to build a similar one for himself.

He chose the top of Talcott Mountain for his site—an elevation of 875 feet. Heublein's six-storied structure originally housed eight bedrooms, each with its own lavatory, fireplace and closet. The ground floor featured a living room, foyer and study, and the top floor served as both a ballroom and observation tower. Heublein used the tower as a summer retreat for his family and friends and many wonderful parties and outings were held here over the years.

After Heublein's death in 1937, the tower with its approximately 350 acres was purchased by Frances S. Murphy, general manager of the *Hartford Times,* a leading Connecticut newspaper. It was used for several years as a broadcast station for the newspaper's radio station, WTHT. During this time it became known as the Times Tower, but the crew and staff who worked on this windy, isolated mountaintop (particularly in the winter) called it The Monastery.

It was also, during this period, the scene of many lively parties and functions frequented by many celebrities of the day such as Dwight D. Eisenhower, Frank Lloyd Wright, Omar Bradley, Admiral Nimitz and many popular movie stars including Ronald Reagan. An enormous barbecue pit was specially built on the grounds to host a large party for General Eisenhower during his presidential campaign.

When the property was put up for sale in 1962, it was purchased by a syndicate for the purpose of developing the tower into a restaurant and building apartments and houses on the property. Citizens from the neighboring towns of Bloomfield, Avon and Simsbury actively fought the project, urging the state to buy the property. "Save Talcott Mountain" soon became the slogan of supporters who were instrumental in bringing about the purchase of the property and its donation to the state of Connecticut for use as a public park.

Since then, aided by a very supportive and active group, The Friends of Heublein Tower, Inc., the tower and surrounding lands have undergone extensive restoration, providing recreational enjoyment for outdoor enthusiasts. No cars are allowed on the mountain (except for staff vehicles), so the only way to get to this scenic spot is on foot. From the parking area, a 1¼-mile trail leads up to the top. For the first quartermile the path is fairly steep and rutted, but there are benches along the way so you can stop and rest. About halfway up, the path winds along the mountain ridge, opening up wonderful vistas of the surrounding countryside.

The tower itself is another climb (there are no ele-

Scenic Sites Near the Tower

There are additional scenic hiking trails and biking paths in the area—Penwood State Park and Stratton Brook State Park.

The entrance to the 787-acre Penwood State Park is just across the road from the Heublein Tower entrance. The scenic Metacomet Trail, part of the Connecticut Blue Trail system, traverses the park. From the park's 741-foot peak elevation there are beautiful panoramic views of both the Connecticut and Farmington river valleys.

Stratton Brook, originally called Massacoe State Forest, was acquired by the state years ago to demonstrate forest fire control adjacent to railroads. The railroad tracks are gone now, but in their place is an excellent bike trail shaded by white pines and traveling over babbling brooks. For information on either park call 203-566-2304.

In nearby Avon is the Horse Cavalry Museum at Riverdale Farms. On most Thursdays from 7:30 to 9:30 P.M., you can watch the Governor's Horse Guards (the oldest cavalry in the country) practice its precision drills. Call 203-673-3525 for more information.

vators), but the view from the top is spectacular. The ballroom/observation tower has been completely restored. The newly stained oak walls display mounted photos that show the room during the time the Heubleins lived there. The living room on the first floor, also restored and partially furnished, exhibits early photos of the area. An extensive picnic grove at the summit is available for group outings.

A spinning wheel still waits in the Russsell-Colbath House for the husband who went out for a walk and never came home.

Little Houses/Tall Tales

All old houses have stories to tell. And since we can't get the walls to talk, we rely on a storyteller to give us the "best" version of the story of a house. For houses that are open to the public, the storytellers are often the docents, who also guide you through the house. They are delightful to listen to, as each one spices up the documented evidence with their favorite anecdotes about the house, its residents and guests.

Purists object to these anecdotes, insisting that the truth is tantamount to historic preservation. Yet it is these stories, whether fact or fancy, that have become a part of Yankee folklore. And the stories are also part of what make these houses so intriguing.

The stories included in this chapter are some of the best that New England has to offer. Although every story is subject to interpretation, we offer them as more fact than fancy.

The Hermit Woman

Kancamagus Highway (12 miles west of Conway) Lincoln, N.H. No phone.

OPEN:
Late June–
Labor Day
Daily: 10–4

ADMISSION:
Free.

The Russell-Colbath House

Lincoln, New Hampshire

1832

One autumn day in 1891, as Ruth Colbath was preparing dinner, her husband Tom called out to her from the backyard saying that he would be back in "a little while." She caught sight of him swinging down the hillside toward the road—and that was to be the last time she would ever see him again.

Ruth, born in 1849, was an intelligent, upstanding woman. For many years she was the Postmistress of Passaconoway. She lived all her life in a cottage that was built by her grandfather in the early 1800s. This was one of the few dwellings along the Kankamagus Pass, a route that is nestled between Mt. Passaconoway and Mt. Chocorua in the White Mountains of New Hampshire. Ruth and Tom were living in Lincoln with Ruth's elderly mother at the time of Tom's disappearance. When her mother died a few years later, Ruth continued to live by herself in the lonely mountain retreat. Each night at sundown, she would place a small lamp in the window to light the way home for Tom.

Years passed, and Ruth kept up her lonely vigil. A few neighbors and relatives visited her occasionally, but no one could ever convince her that Tom was never coming back. She stayed on alone, living in her house through the deadliest of winters, placing the light in the window each night and never giving up hope for his return. She stopped leaving her home, and eventually became known along the Kankamagus Pass as the "hermit woman." Although she welcomed the few visitors who passed her way, she refused to answer any questions about the lamp in the window.

Ruth died alone in 1930. Just three years after her death, Tom Colbath returned to Lincoln. He was

a bit vague about where he had been for 42 years and why he left, but told a neighbor about his travels to such faraway places as Cuba, Panama and California. When he was told about his wife's lonely 39-year vigil, Tom hung his head in sorrow and disbelief.

The Russell-Colbath House serves as a visitors' center to campers, hikers and picnickers.

Tom moved back into the deserted house and lived there for his few remaining years—alone.

The small 1½-story wood-frame Cape house is now a prominent landmark along the famous Kancamagus Highway. It has been restored by the U.S. Forest Service with nineteenth-century furnishings, and is still one of the few houses along this now-historic roadway. It serves as a visitors' center where rangers provide information to campers, hikers and picnickers who flock to this scenic area. The story of Ruth Colbath is prominently displayed on one of the walls and the Rangers are continuously asked about her.

The Kanc

Legend has it that Kancamagus (meaning "The Fearless One") was the name of the final Sagamon (chief) of the Penacook Confederacy—one of the early Indian tribes that ruled this area of the White Mountains. He was said to be peace-loving, but eventually war and bloodshed with other tribes and pioneering whites scattered his tribe to the north, probably to Canada.

Legendary or not, his name has come to mean to many vacationers to this spectacular area one of the most scenic highways in New England. Locals have shortened the name to "the Kanc." What were once a couple of old lumbering railbeds were merged into a winding, paved highway in the mid-1940s. This made it possible to traverse the flank of Mt. Kancamagus (climbing to nearly 3,000 feet) at Lincoln and drive to Conway—a distance of 34½ miles.

Along the way there are several "overlooks" (parking spots with great panoramic views), picnic areas (with drinking water and sanitary stations) and hiking trails (trail maps are available at the visitor center). There are also campgrounds, with most campsites available on a first-come basis. Limited reservations are accepted at Covered Bridge Campground (call 1-800-283-CAMP). For further information about recreational activities along the Kancamagus Highway call 603-528-8721.

Grandpapa Gilley

The Blossom House
Monmouth, Maine
1800

Route 132
Monmouth Center
Monmouth, Maine
207-933-4911

OPEN:
Memorial Day–
October 1
Tues–Sun: 1-4
and by appointment

ADMISSION:
Donation requested.

The story of John Gilley has become a legend in Maine. Not only is his story well documented in local history books, he also has hundreds of descendents— who gather for a family reunion each summer—who can attest to its authenticity. Gilley even made it into the famous "Ripley's Believe It or Not" column many years ago. His feat? Not only did he live to be 124 years old, but he married for the first time at the age of 80 and fathered 10 children.

Gilley immigrated to America from Ireland in 1755. He enlisted in the army at Fort Western on the Kennebec River in Maine. The commander of the fort, Captain James Howard, was at first skeptical of this "runty little Irishman." Gilley was only five feet, three inches tall, and was about 65 years old at that time. Upon seeing him, Howard exclaimed that he probably couldn't even "bring a barrel of bread from the shore."

John proved him wrong, and served at the fort for 15 years. He left at the age of 80 only to settle down and get married. He won the heart of Dorcas Brawn, a 24-year-old lass who called him "Grandpapa Gilley." They bought a farm where John did all his own plowing. Dorcas proceeded to have one baby after another for the next 20 years—10 children in all. John was 100 years old at the birth of his tenth child.

As John continued to age, he remained strong in body and mind. He began to confound not only historians, but doctors as well. He was examined closely by Dr. Benjamin Vaughan of Hallowell, Maine, a highly respected physician in the area. Dr. Vaughan concluded that he was "satisfied that [John's] age was not overstated." Also, at the same time, the noted Maine historian James W. North conceded that, from all accounts, John Gilley was indeed born about 1689 or 1690 in Ireland, near Cork.

John enjoyed good health and a sound mind, and he remained active until the end of his life. When asked to what he attributed his longevity, he candidly replied, "meat three times a day."

When he died in 1813, two doctors, with a judge in attendance, made a post-mortem examination of the body. They were so amazed by the good condition of his organs that they sent them off to Harvard Medical School for further study. (The family joked that John

The desk of John Gilley, who fathered ten children after his eightieth birthday.

was the only Gilley to make it to Harvard.)

The Gilley farm, which was located about three miles from the fort, is no longer standing, but the old fort itself, now a National Landmark, is well preserved and is now part of the Fort Western Museum.

The Monmouth Museum in nearby Monmouth, Maine, is the repository for one of the few tangible assets (aside from the prolific number of descendents) left by John. It is his wooden desk, where he must have spent long hours figuring out the finances for his large family. The Blossom House, built shortly after the town of Monmouth was incorporated, is presently being restored to its original condition. It represents a typical farmhouse of the period, such as the Gilleys might have lived in.

The Oldest Fort in New England

When John Gilley came to Fort Western in Agusta, Maine, to enlist in the army in 1775, the fort was only a year old. As early as 1625, however, Pilgrims from Plymouth colony had visited here at the Indian village of Cushnoc (now Augusta) and set up a trading post with the Abenaki Indians. The site was ideally located at the head of the navigable portion of the Kennebec River.

During the outbreak of the French and Indian wars, the settlers withdrew and didn't return until 1754. At that time they built the fort to protect the new permanent settlement of the upper Kennebec Valley. Following the threat of hostilities, the fort's commander, James Howard, purchased the fort and surrounding land. Rapid growth in the region soon followed and Fort Western became a hub of activity, serving as meeting house, church, trading post, business office and residence.

As the city of Augusta grew in stature, the fort fell into disuse. Restoration began in 1919 to save this historic relic and was completed in 1922. Since then it has served as a city museum. It is the oldest surviving colonial proprietary fort in New England and its collections and displays in 14 rooms interpret the social, political and economic history of the area. Call 207-289-2301 for more information.

Duston House

Haverhill, Massachusetts

1 6 8 5

665 Hillside Avenue
Haverhill, Mass.
508-374-4626

OPEN:
Annually in August
during the Duston-
Dustin Garrison
House Association
meeting.

In the spring of 1697, residents of the frontier village of Haverhill were constantly on the lookout for Indians. An early thaw had caused the ice to break on the Merrimack River, thus creating easy access for small war parties of Abernakis who descended the river from the north whenever it ran free. In the event of an attack, the bell outside the meetinghouse was rung. Even the smallest child in the village had been trained to rush to the nearest garrison at the sound of the bell.

On the western outskirts of town, Thomas Duston and his three older children were clearing a field of rocks. He could not see a small band of Indians, daubed with war paint, emerging from the woods behind his small farmhouse. Inside the house, his wife Hannah was nursing her newborn child. A neighbor, Mary Neff, was there helping to care for mother, baby and the three younger Duston children.

With ferocious suddenness, the warriors burst into the house. Mary was immediately struck by a tomahawk and badly wounded. Two Indians pushed into the bedroom, grabbed the baby from its mother's arms and flung it against the wall, killing it instantly. Dazed and shocked, Hannah was pulled from her bed and dragged into the kitchen, where she was forced to lie beside Mary while the Indians ransacked the house. They quickly packed up what they wanted, then dragged the two women with them as they left the house, which they burned.

Meanwhile, the three small children had managed to elude their captors, and ran screaming from the house into the fields toward their father. Thomas Duston, seeing his frightened children with two Indians close on their heels, grabbed his musket and began to fire. The Indians quickly retreated, running back toward the burning house. Duston, fearing his wife and Mary were dead, gathered up his six children and ran for the garrison.

When Duston and the children arrived at the garrison, they learned that the whole village had been attacked in force. The attack had been swift but brutal—27 people were dead and 13 were taken captive. Hannah Duston and Mary Neff were among the captives.

The attackers, loaded down with their bounty and slowed by their captives, divided up into small groups to make their way north along the Merrimac. Hannah and Mary, along with a young boy named Samuel Lenorson, were sent with four warriors, a squaw and six Indian children. The three were constantly harassed and threatened by their captors.

After 45 days of living in the wilds—hungry, tired and constantly fearing for their lives—the three captives began to hatch a daring escape plan. Before retiring that night, Hannah managed to steal a tomahawk from one of the unsuspecting guards. In the dark of the early morning hours, Hannah and her

This is the home that Thomas Duston was building when his wife, Hannah, was captured by indians.

two accomplices crept silently up to the sleeping warriors. With lightning speed, Hannah wielded her hatchet. Not only did she manage to kill her captors, but she scalped them as well.

The three then made their long trek back to Haverhill with the scalps of their victims rolled up in a deerskin, where they were joyfully greeted and honored as heroes. In fact, the General Court of Massachusetts voted to give Hannah 25 pounds, as well as 12 pounds 10 shillings each to Mary Neff and Samuel Lenorson "for the scalps of public enemies."

The Poet's Home

Besides Hannah Duston's house, there are several more seventeenth-century houses in the city of Haverhill, but probably none of them more well known than the birthplace of famed poet John Greenleaf Whittier. It was built in 1688 by his great-great-grandfather, Thomas Whittier, beside a bubbling brook that furnished enough water for his farm needs and to turn his mill wheel. The homestead is a fine example of early New England farmhouses, and the farm has been in continual operation since the days of Thomas.

The house and it environs are the setting for Whittier's classic poem "Snowbound," as well as many of his early works. With few exceptions, it remains as it was when Whittier lived there as a boy, although a fire in 1901 nearly destroyed the upper level of the house. It was immediately restored by the Haverhill-Whittier Club, which has managed the house since 1898.

After his father's death in 1836, Whittier moved to the nearby town of Amesbury with his mother and sister (to be closer to the Quaker Meeting House) and lived in the same house for almost 50 years. It was here that most of his best-loved poems were written. The house has been preserved as it was at the time of his death and is filled with all his personal belongings. Visitors enjoy seeing the desk on which Whittier wrote his celebrated poetry as well as nearly 100 hymns, and where he compiled and edited a number of books and edited and wrote for antislavery journals. His birthplace, 305 Whittier Road, Haverhill (508-373-3979), and his home, 86 Friend Street, Amesbury, (508-388-1337) are both open to the public.

A small brick Colonial home, said to be the one Thomas Duston was building at the time of his wife's capture, is one of the very few seventeenth-century brick houses still standing. It has undergone many restorations and suffered through two fires, but still retains some of its original features. Called a "half-house" because the location of the main door is off to one side, it is owned and maintained by the Duston-Dustin Garrison House Association. Annual family reunions are held here every August to honor Hannah Duston.

A statue of Hannah wielding a tomahawk has been erected in a local park. The tomahawk and scalping knife that Hannah used are on view at the Haverhill Historical Society Museum.

The Recluse

21 Elm Street
Rockland, Maine
207-596-6457

OPEN:
June 1–
mid-September
Mon–Sat: 10–5
Sun: 1–5

Farnsworth Homestead

Rockland, Maine

1840

Lucy Farnsworth was a woman ahead of her time. In an age when the typical girl from a wealthy family married, had children, took care of her house and joined all the right clubs, Lucy rebelled. She did none of the expected things. And why should she? She was smarter than her brothers, her father preferred discussing his business matters with her, she knew how to play the stock market and, when the need arose, she could argue her own case in court—almost always with great success. Lucy could take care of herself.

By not bowing to convention, however, Lucy was thought of as odd and eccentric. The stories that circulated around town about her became legend, and many of them had to do with her miserly ways. She went to court rather than pay a lawyer his $10 fee for collecting a mortgage payment for her. (It was one of the few cases she lost.) She once sent a boy to buy ten cents of meat for her cat, then sent him to return it because, in the interim, the cat had caught a rat. Her father had left her a sizeable inheritance, but Lucy never spent any money to electrify her house. He also left her his two-horse surrey, and when one of the horses died, she converted the surrey to one-horse. When that horse died, she walked.

After her father's death, Lucy lived alone with her mother in their large, comfortable home on Elm Street in Rockland, Maine. The two women did not get along very well, as is evidenced by the kitchen stove. It was a dual stove, made especially for them with two ovens and two cooking surfaces so they could cook separately. Mrs. Farnsworth died in 1910 at the age of 94 and, as all the other siblings had passed away, Lucy became the sole heir to the family

The formal parlor of the Farnsworth home.

fortune, estimated to be about $225,000 at that time.

After her mother's death Lucy stayed more to herself than ever, eventually becoming a recluse. When she did appear in town on necessary errands she wore an old, outdated black dress and long black coat, a peaked black bonnet and a black veil; she carried a black handbag. A formidable figure, she spoke only when necessary and few dared approach her.

On two separate occasions, Lucy's milkman became alarmed when her milk bottles began piling up on the back doorstep. When he called the fire department to investigate, Lucy, sick in bed, hurled obscenities at them and told them to leave her alone.

On the morning of October 15, 1935, the bottles were piled up for a third time. The milkman had a premonition that all was not well and alerted the town marshal. The two of them entered the house and found Lucy dead in her bed. The condition of the house was shocking. Every room was covered with a thick layer of dust and dirt. Books and papers were piled up everywhere. The dining room table was piled high with bank statements, brokers' receipts, rent receipts, checks, stock market reports—and money.

Money, in fact, was to be found everywhere—piled on tables, stuffed in drawers, hidden under carpets and dumped into a large bowl in the middle of the dining room table. Under the stair runners, they found thousands of dollars in stocks and bonds. When it was all counted up by the proper authorities, Lucy's estate totaled over $1,500,000.

Lucy's will, also found in the house, proved to be the biggest surprise of all. She bequeathed her entire fortune to the establishment of an art center and library in Rockport in honor of her father. She also stated in her will that she wished her house to be maintained as it had been in her lifetime.

Local Color

The Farnsworth Art Museum, adjacent to the Farnsworth Homestead in Rockland, Maine, is considered to be one of finest regional art museums in the country. The first art museum in the state to be accredited by the American Association of Museums, it has gained in stature and popularity since it opened its doors in 1948.

Its permanent collection contains strong holdings in European paintings as well as European and Oriental art objects. It is particularly rich in American art and decorative arts from the eighteenth, nineteenth and twentieth centuries. The Farnsworth prides itself on its works by artists from New England, particularly those from Maine. Most favored by visitors to the museum is the Farnsworth Maine Heritage Collection, focusing on art created in Maine from the eighteenth century to the present. Familiar Maine scenes evoke cherished memories in the works of Winslow Homer, Fitz Hugh Lane, Fairfield Porter, Rockwell Kent, George Bellows and, of course, N.C., Andrew and Jamie Wyeth. (The Farnsworth owns one of the largest collections of Andrew Wyeth paintings.)

The museum's archives, available to scholars, contain valuable material on many artists who had strong connections to Maine. The museum is open year-round. Call 207-596-6457 for information.

The handsome Greek Revival Farnsworth Homestead has been preserved exactly as it was in the nineteenth century (sans dust and dirt!). It is now considered one of the finest Victorian-era residences on the east coast. It was placed on the National Register of Historic Places in 1972.

The William A. Farnsworth Library and Art Museum ranks among the finest regional art museums in the country. It is noted for its collection of American art by well-known regional artists such as N. C., Andrew and Jamie Wyeth; Louise Nevelson and George Bellows.

To this day, the story amazes both townspeople and visitors to Rockland. Lucy, a little old eccentric lady known for her miserly, reclusive nature, surprised them all with her generous bequest.

The door of John Sheldon's house, with evidence of the famous tomahawk attack.

Scenes of Dastardly Deeds

Witchcraft, Indian massacres, hatchet murders, disappearing towns and so-called mad scientists are all part of the otherwise calm New England scene. Behind those gray-shingled Colonial cottages and native stone structures all manner of travesties have been carried out, bringing everlasting fame to some of our historical dwellings.

Visitors flock to these houses because of curiosity or fascination with the macabre, but they leave with a deeper understanding of American history—the time and place in which these events occurred. Witchcraft and Indian massacres are a thing of the past and presumably, so is labeling a scientist "mad." Towns are rarely destroyed these days, but crimes of passion will be with us forever.

The Deerfield Massacre

The Street
Deerfield, Mass.
413-774-7476

OPEN:
May 1–October 31
Mon–Fri: 10–4:30
Sat–Sun: 12:30–4:30

ADMISSION:
Inquire for prices.

The Old Indian House

Deerfield, Massachusetts

1 6 9 8

During the period of hostilities between France and Great Britain for overseas rule, which started in 1689 and led up to the French and Indian War (1754-63), the residents of the small town of Deerfield, Massachusetts, did not usually sleep well. Their little farming village, crouched on the most northern boundary of the Commonwealth, was a lonely and poorly fortified outpost. Settlers were subjected to constant threats, sudden attacks and vicious pillaging by warring Indian tribes.

Farther to the north, along the disputed border between French Canada and the English settlements in Maine and New Hampshire, hostilities between the French and English were constantly erupting. Both sides enlisted the aid of various Indian tribes. And, although the small outpost of Deerfield had been prone to Indian attacks in the past, it had been almost 30 years since the last bloody battle, in which 64 men—17 from Deerfield—were masssacred.

But now, on a bitter cold February night in 1704, the nearly 300 residents of the town slept peacefully—including the sentry at his post. The snow had been falling for days, and a 300-mile area was buried, from Deerfield north to the border.

Unbeknownst to the residents, an army of 200 French soldiers and 142 Indians—under the command of Hertel de Rouville and sent by the governor of Canada—was marching across the vast frozen wilderness toward their village. This army's plan was to plunder Deerfield and capture prisoners to take back to Canada. They arrived on the outskirts of the village before daybreak and waited in a low ravine for their opportunity to storm the stockade.

At first light, aided by the snow piled high against

the stockade wall, the invaders swarmed over the wall and into the town. Guns and hatchets raised high, they war-whooped through the village, plundering, murdering, capturing prisoners and burning houses as they went.

In one instance, at the stoutly built and heavily studded door of John Sheldon's house, their hatchets met with fierce resistance. It took several tomahawk blows to finally make a gash in the door, and one shouting warrior pushed the barrel of a gun through the hole. He fired blindly, killing Mrs. Sheldon, who was just rising from her bed. From the second-floor bedroom, her son John and his young bride Hannah jumped to safety, but Hannah injured her foot in the fall. She pleaded with her husband to go ahead without her and get help. Young John, though lightly clad, was able to flee 14 miles away to Hatfield, where he sounded the alarm and sent help back to Deerfield.

Captured prisoners, most of them clad only in nightclothes, were rounded up and kept under guard at the Sheldon house while the raiders continued to plunder and burn as many houses as they could. The leader of the raid, de Rouville, fearing the fires would

Period costumes and well-preserved structures add to the authenticity of historic Deerfield and the Old Indian House.

soon be seen for some distance, ordered his men to quickly pile the stolen provisions from the villagers' homes and stores onto wagons. Then, herding the prisoners—111 men, women and children—they began the 300-mile trek back to Canada.

The march was a torturous ordeal for the captives. Without proper clothes and shoes, many became sick and died along the way. According to an eyewitness account by the village minister, Reverend John Williams, "Their manner was, if any loitered, to kill them." The first to be so punished was a three-year-old child, Marah Carter, who straggled behind. Williams' own wife, frail in health, was felled by a blow from a tomahawk after she stumbled and fell. Pregnant Mary Brooks, unable to keep pace, soon met with the same fate.

Besides the 111 captives, 49 English settlers were killed and the village nearly devastated. Only half the population remained: 25 men, 25 women and 75 young children.

As those that remained set about rebuilding the village, John Sheldon, senior, who had survived the attack but lost most of his family, was determined to bring the captured villagers home. He obtained a commission from the governor of Massachusetts to set out on foot with a guide to bargain with the governor of Canada for the return of the prisoners.

The first spring he brought back five, including his daughter-in-law, Hannah, and in two subsequent trips, he was able to bring back most of the remaining captives. The negotiations took three years, however, and during that time some of the captives, particularly the young children, were adopted into native tribes and preferred to remain there.

The home of John Sheldon, built in 1698, was one of the few surviving houses of the infamous massacre. It became known as the Old Indian House and, in spite of one of the first attempts at preservation in New England, it was demolished in 1847. The front door of the house, still bearing the scars left by tomahawks, was saved. It, along with some other mementos of the house, is on display at Memorial Hall Museum. The present Old Indian House is an exact replica of John Sheldon's house. It was built to specifications in 1929 as a gift of William H. Abercrombie in memory of the Deerfield pioneers.

Today, Deerfield is regarded as one of the most beautiful and well-preserved villages in America. "The Street," as the mile-long thoroughfare running through the center of town is called, is lined with well over a dozen historical museum houses. Built in the eighteenth and nineteenth centuries and filled with priceless antiques, many of them are open to the public throughout the year.

Time Travel in Deerfield

Historic Deerfield, no longer prone to savage Indian attacks, was founded in 1952 by Mr. and Mrs. Henry N. Flynt "to carry on the tradition of historic preservation in this picturesque western Massachusetts village." The foundation maintains 11 house museums, a research library and an active education program, all devoted to the study of the history of Deerfield, the culture of the Connecticut Valley and Early American arts.

The first place to stop when visiting here is the visitor's information center at Hall Tavern, where you can obtain general information and purchase tickets. A brochure describing each of the houses, its history and its furnishings is available; guided tours are given. A nice house to visit if you are bringing children is The Frary House, with its special "touch it" room.

Some of the houses and buildings are devoted to special exhibits. The Parker and Russell Silver Shop displays an outstanding collection of American and English silver. The Wilson Printing House is restored to its original site and is used as a printing office and book bindery. The Helen Geier Flynt Fabric Hall is actually a Victorian barn with a remarkable collection of American, English and European needlework, textiles and costumes of the seventeenth, eighteenth and nineteenth centuries. The museum houses and buildings are open throughout the year, except for major holidays. For information call 413-773-5401.

Lizzie Borden Took an Ax

451 Rock Street
Fall River, Mass.
617-679-1071

OPEN:
March–December
Tues–Fri: 9–4:30
Sat–Sun: 1–5
Closed holidays.

ADMISSION:
Inquire for prices.

Brayton House

Fall River, Massachusetts
1 8 4 3

Probably no murder in the annals of American crime has received as much attention as that of the Borden family of Fall River, Massachusetts. In the summer of 1892, Lizzie Borden, a 32-year-old Sunday school teacher and daughter of a wealthy and prominent family in Fall River, was accused of hacking to death her father and stepmother. At that time, her highly publicized trial—with all the gory murder details revealed—was telegraphed around the world to an insatiable audience. When, after 15 days, the prosecution was unable to produce a witness, a murder weapon or a clear reason for the murders, it took the all-male jury little more than an hour to acquit her.

But speculation about her guilt has long remained, perpetuated by the childhood rhyme:

Lizzie Borden took an ax
Gave her mother forty whacks;
When she saw what she had done
She gave her father forty-one.

It happened on a hot August morning in 1892. Lizzie Borden, the younger of the two Borden sisters, was downstairs in the locked house at 92 Second Street. The housemaid, Bridget, was outside washing windows; Emma, Lizzie's older sister, was visiting friends in a nearby town. The only other person in the house was Amy Borden, Lizzie's stepmother, who was upstairs tidying up the guest bedroom.

Someone, in those sultry late morning hours, managed to enter the tightly locked house and brutally hack Mrs. Borden to death without anyone hearing a thing. And 1½ hours later, Mr. Borden, returning from work and entering his study for a quick nap before

lunch, was similarly murdered on the sofa.

As the investigation proceeded, suspicion began to build against Lizzie. No one had been seen entering or leaving the house. It was no secret that she hated her stepmother and was afraid her father was being influenced by her. But in the idealistic, Victorian climate of the late 1800s, it was unthinkable that a respectable young woman from one of the town's founding families could perpetrate such a heinous crime.

When Lizzie was arrested, sentiment was strongly in her favor. Soon after her acquittal, feelings changed. After the trial, the two sisters purchased a grand house, which Lizzie named Maplecroft. It was in the fashionable section of Fall River, but the Borden sisters soon found that they were no longer welcome in that society. Over the years, former friends began to stop coming to the big house. The women did little entertaining and, for the most part, kept to themselves. Lizzie began to make the acquaintance of "theatre people," much to the horror of her sister, and often invited actors and actresses to their home. Finally one night, Emma mysteriously left the house in a fury and never returned.

Lizzie died from complications of a gall bladder operation on June 2, 1927, with only her maids and cats for company. Eight days later, her sister Emma, living as a recluse in New Hampshire, died after falling down a flight of stairs and breaking her hip. Their graves, marked by two simple stones and engraved with their first names (Lizzie had changed her name to "Lisbeth" after her trial) lie side by side in the Borden plot in Oak Grove Cemetery.

The house at 92 Second Street (now 230 Second Street), a plain, modest, three-story house that Lizzie hated, still stands, now occupied by a print shop. Maplecroft, on French Street, is privately owned.

The Brayton House on Rock Street is home to the Fall River Historical Society and it is here that the the world-famous Lizzie Borden exhibit can be seen. Memorabilia on display includes Lizzie's supper pail from the Taunton jail, Mrs. Borden's braided wiglet and dusting cap, photos of the skulls of Andrew and Abby Borden showing the large gashes made by the ax, the infamous handleless hatchet (never proven to be the murder weapon), a blood-spattered bedspread, some personal items of Lizzie's, many tagged exhibits from the trial and a section of the railing from the courtroom.

The Brayton House is one of the few surviving mansions built by the affluent mill owners who prospered in Fall River when it was the largest cloth-making city in the world. The mansion was built of Fall River granite in 1843 for mill scion Andrew Robeson, Jr., and originally stood next to his mill near the river. At one point, it was used as a station of the Underground Railroad for escaping slaves, and the entrance to a secret passageway is still visible in the built-in bookcases. In 1870, as lifestyles changed, it was moved, with each piece of stone marked and dragged by oxen up to the more desirable section of town on the hill (not far from Maplecroft), where it was carefully reconstructed.

Freetown's Cotton

While the collection of Lizzie Borden memorabilia is one of the most sought-out attractions at the Fall River Historical Museum, the guides here strive amiably to give visitors a real sense of the city's proud history.

Fall River was settled in 1656, and was then known as Freetown. It was formally founded in 1803 and was incorporated as a city in 1854. Situated at the mouth of the Taunton River, which provided it with an excellent harbor and access to water power, it became the foremost cotton textile center in the United States in the nineteenth century. Immigrants from many countries poured into the city to work in the mills, giving Fall River a rich cultural heritage.

Today, many of the old mills, built of granite quarried from the ledges on which much of the city was built, still stand in mute testimony to those more prosperous times. Some of them, however, do not stand idle—they have been transformed into a major factory-outlet shopping center. The Heart District, where most of the outlets are located, features over 100 money-saving factory outlets. It has the distinction of being the largest factory outlet in New England. Busloads of eager shoppers arrive daily from all over New England to take advantage of great discounts on clothing, furniture and household items. For information call 508-678-6033.

Battleship Cove at the State Pier is another of Fall River's main attractions. Guided tours of World War II vessels such as the *USS Massachusetts* and the *Joseph P. Kennedy, Jr.*, are given. Next to Battleship Cove is Fall River State Park, an eight-acre park with a vistors' center and a variety of exhibits on Fall River's textile and nautical history. There is also a slide presentation on the city's role as a major cotton textile producer. For information call 508-678-1100.

Witchcraft

149 Pine Street
Danvers, Mass.
No phone.

OPEN:
Mid-June–
mid-October
Tues–Sat: 1–4:30
Sun: 2–4:30
and by appointment

ADMISSION:
Inquire for prices.

The Rebecca Nurse House
Danvers, Massachusetts
1 6 7 8

In the seventeenth century, Danvers, Massachusetts, was known as Salem Village. It was here that the infamous witch trials took place in 1692. It was a time of social and political unrest in the colony, with petty land disputes and religious differences setting villagers against one another. The climate was ripe for the events that were to follow.

The Reverend Samuel Parris had left his unsuccessful business ventures in the West Indies to accept a call to the village church in Salem. Not all of the members approved of this stern Puritan as their minister and the choice caused a split in the congregation. Nevertheless, he arrived in the throes of a bitter-cold winter with his wife Elizabeth and two children—a seven-year-old daughter, Betty, and a precocious twelve-year-old neice, Abigail. He also brought two Jamaican slaves, Tituba and John.

In the ensuing dreary months, with only the household chores and the reading of scriptures to occupy their time, the girls grew restless. When the girls' parents were away, Tituba began to entertain them by reading their palms and telling fortunes. She told them stories of spectres, witches and Caribbean natives who practiced mysterious acts of voodoo.

Soon other young girls in the village were secretly gathering at the parsonage to listen to Tituba's exciting stories. At their insistence, she began to teach them "black magic." They learned to put themselves into a "trance"—their bodies twisted and contorted and they uttered strange sounds.

While Abigail and the older girls were thrilled with these games, the younger girls, particularly Betty, became terrified. She and some of the others began having nightmares and falling into uncontrollable fits at

The modest home of Rebecca Nurse.

any given time. In the days to follow, the alarmed and unsuspecting parents called in a doctor to examine the children. Unable to determine any known malady, he diagnosed them as being under the spell of witches.

All of the girls became truly frightened. They knew that witchcraft was a very serious crime. Puritans believed strongly in the power of witches and devils, and anyone caught practicing witchcraft was put to death. When they were brought, shaking and hysterical, before the village elders and commanded to reveal their tormentors, they pointed to Tituba and two other poor, elderly village women. The three women were immediately seized and thrown into jail.

In the months to follow, urged on by their elders, the girls began to name others. Many of the accused were enemies of the Reverend Parris. One such person was Rebecca Nurse, the 71-year-old matriarch of a large and prominent family. She was one of the first to doubt the girls' truthfulness and was heard to say that those accused of witchcraft "were as innocent as" she was.

Ann Putnam, one of the "afflicted" girls and the daughter of a family who had a long, unsettled land dispute with the Nurse family, was quick to point an accusing finger at Rebecca. Constables went to the Nurse homestead, plucked Rebecca from her sick bed, arrested her and threw her into a filthy jail cell.

The villagers were outraged. A petition was circulated on Rebecca's behalf. When Rebecca was brought to trial, she stood before the magistrate and calmly professed her innocence:

As to this thing, I am innocent as the child unborn, but surely what sin hath God found out in me unrepented of that He should lay such an affliction upon me in my old age?

Impressed by her words, the jury found her innocent of the charges. But as she was excused, the "afflicted" girls, sitting in the front row of the courtroom, fell onto the floor and began to scream and writhe in terror. The presiding magistrate was so horrified by what he saw that he quickly asked the jury to reconsider. And so they did—reversing their decision.

Rebecca's family and friends continued to fight to save her life, but within a short time she was hanged on Gallows Hill in Salem. Her body was placed in a nearby common grave. During the night, her sons secretly dug up and removed her body, burying her in the family plot behind the Nurse homestead.

The witch trials were finally brought to an end in the spring of 1693, after 19 people were hanged and one man "pressed" to death. Fourteen years later, Ann Putnam stood up in the village church and apologized for her acts. She admitted that none of the things she said were true, and that she had been tricked into saying them by the devil.

In 1885 the Nurse family erected a memorial to Rebecca in the family graveyard. The inscription was written by famed poet John Greenleaf Whittier:

O Christian Martyr, who for truth could die
When all about thee owned the hideous lie,
The world, redeemed from Superstition's sway,
Is breathing freer for thy sake today.

Later, another marker dedicated to the 40 neighbors who signed her petition of innocence was erected nearby.

An old dirt road leads to the ancient saltbox-style Nurse homestead. Behind the house is the old family graveyard with its solemn headstones. The house contains three restored rooms with period furnishings of the seventeenth and eighteenth centuries, giving a visible link to the period during and following the infamous witch trials.

The land remained in the Nurse family for many

Rebecca's Neighborhood

One of the early settlers of Salem Village (Danvers) was Benjamin Holton, who built his house on property adjoining that of Rebecca Nurse. The Holton family was related to the Putnams, who also had a home nearby. Members of these two families, embroiled in land disputes, were among those that accused Rebecca of being a witch, and gave damaging testimony at her trial.

The Holton house is a typical early Colonial home, a two-room house with a large central chimney and stairs at the end leading to an attic room. Continuing generations of Holtons lived in the house for more than 200 years, and many additions have been made to it. The house is furnished with many historic pieces and personal items of the Holton family. It is now owned by the Daughters of the American Revolution, who maintain it as a house museum. It is open on special occasions. For a schedule and information call 508-777-1666.

Two other interesting houses of a later period are also in this neighborhood. The Jeremiah Page House (1754) and Glen Magna (1814) are both maintained as historical house museums by the Danvers Historical Society. Glen Magna, the former summer estate of the Peabody and Endicott families, is particularly nice to visit in the summer with its formal gardens and park-like setting. The Page House was home to three generations of the Page family, the last of whom was Ann Page. Ann operated one of the earliest kindergarten programs in the country—in this house. The house is filled with Page family mementos and many local historical artifacts. Call 508-774-9165 for information.

years. Ironically, it was purchased by members of the Putnam family in 1784. It remained in that family until 1908, when it was purchased and restored by the Rebecca Nurse Memorial Association. In 1981, it was taken over by the present owners, Danvers Alarm List Company, Inc., a re-created eighteenth-century Massachusetts militia unit. Throughout the year (for historical programs), the company portrays the seventeeth-century militia, alarm companies and colonial life of the town of Danvers. The group is highly acclaimed, and has performed for the Queen of England, as well as the presidents of both France and the United States.

The Accumulator

Orgonon

Rangeley, Maine
1951

Dodge Pond Road
Rangeley, Maine
207-864-3443

OPEN:
July–August
Tues–Sun: 1–5

September
Sun: 1–5

ADMISSION:
Inquire for prices.

Dr. Wilhelm Reich's home and laboratory, high in an isolated section of the Rangeley Mountains, is, at first sight, the perfect setting for a gripping thriller. Orgonon is a massive gray fieldstone structure, built in the early Bauhaus style with an observatory and many odd-shaped windows. It dominates a clearing in this wooded 200-acre mountainside location. Winding paths lead off into the dark woods, one of which leads to the highest point on the site. It is here that you will find the tomb of Dr. Reich—a life-size bronze bust atop a large fieldstone monument. The famous Dr. Reich died in 1957 far from his mountaintop retreat—in a prison cell in Pennsylvania.

Reich, a psychoanalyst, was born in Austria in 1897. He was a student of Sigmund Freud, but the two would later come into conflict. Reich's contention that he had discovered a previously unknown form of energy—"orgone"—sounded a note of discord among his colleagues.

In his effort to study and isolate orgone, Reich developed the "Orgone Energy Accumulator." He created it by layering metallic and nonmetallic materials so that they attracted and concentrated the radiating energy in the atmosphere. In order to make it accessible to people, he constructed an accumulator that resembled a short telephone booth. A person could sit inside this accumulator and, Reich contended, charge bodily tissues, particularly the blood supply and other functions. The accumulator functioned as a therapeutic aid, helping to restore the patient's vitality and resistance to disease.

The box attracted the attention of the media and, in turn, the U.S. Food and Drug Administration. In 1954, the FDA labeled the accumulator a fraud and

Wilhelm Reich in his laboratory at Orgonon.

not only filed an injunction to prevent interstate sale and shipment of the accumulator, but banned all of Reich's books (some were burned).

Reich strongly protested this decision, but without success. When one of his students later transported an accumulator over the state line, Reich was charged with criminal contempt and found guilty. He was sentenced to a two-year term in the federal penitentiary in Lewisburg, Pennsylvania. Nine months later, he suffered a heart seizure during the night and died in his bed.

While Reich was ridiculed by many of his colleagues for his orgone theory, there were many more who praised his work and worked for the release of his books and papers, some of which are considered classics in their fields. At the time of his death, it was said that he had treated thousands of patients. Many of these patients had been treated unsuccessfully by other methods, and were willing to testify to the powerful effects of Reich's remarkable therapy.

His former home and laboratory, Orgonon, is now formally called The Wilheim Reich Museum and is used primarily as an educational center where conferences on current scientific, medical and social issues are held. During the summer months there are also many natural science programs and workshops for both adults and children. Visitors can enjoy hiking along the natural history trails on the museum grounds, taking guided tours of the house and laboratory and viewing a slide presentation.

His laboratory, to which he planned to return, has been kept much as it was when he left it: Reich's inventions take up most of the space in the building. Biographical exhibits, scientific equipment, original paintings and sculpture sit side by side with his most controversial creation of all—and the one that landed him in jail—the "Orgone Energy Accumulator."

Vacationland USA

There are so many beautiful places in Maine for vacationing, it's difficult to call one place better than another. But for the outdoor sports enthusiast, the Rangeley Lakes Region—home to Orgonon— definitely ranks among the top. This section of the Appalachians encompasses more than 450 square miles of sweeping pine forests and a chain of clear, sparkling lakes and streams, providing an endless variety of recreational activities—all pollution free.

The area has been famous for years as "the home of the fighting trout and the landlocked salmon," and it lives up to its name. Visitors can enjoy a private rustic log cabin on the edge of a lake (boat included), or a roomy lodge with all the modern amenities. Hunting is also popular here, as are canoeing, hiking, camping, boating and swimming. An 18-hole golf course (at 2,000 feet above sea level) offers a nice challenge, as do the 40 alpine ski trails at the Saddleback ski resort.

Rangeley Lake State Park, located on the east shore of Rangeley Lake, consists of 691 acres of recreation area with swimming, fishing, picnicking, camping and boat-launching facilities.

An all-seasons "Escape Kit" is available from the Rangeley Chamber of Commerce by calling 207-864-5364.

The Lost Towns

Elm Street
New Salem, Mass.
617-544-6807

OPEN:
June–September
Sun: 2–4
Third Saturdays in
June and
September: 11–3
July–August
Wed. 2–4

ADMISSION:
Inquire for prices.
Write: Swift River
Historical Society,
P.O. Box 24, New
Salem, MA 01355.

Whitaker-Clary House

New Salem, Massachusetts
1 8 1 6

On the lawn of the Whitaker-Clary House in the rural residential town of New Salem, Massachusetts, a unique signpost points the way to towns and villages including Dana, Enfield, Greenwich and Prescott. These four towns, however, no longer exist. The memory of them lives on in perpetuity inside the Whitaker-Clary House.

The house serves as headquarters for the Swift River Valley Historical Society, established in 1935 for the purpose of preserving the history and artifacts of these four towns. Between 1939 and 1946, they were intentionally submerged under water to create the Quabbin Reservoir, one of the largest domestic water supplies in the world.

What prompted this drastic move was the rapid growth of Boston and the entire metropolitan area around the turn of the century. The need for a new water supply was great—many of the lakes and rivers in the Boston area had become highly polluted with industrial wastes and sewage. Since the early 1800s, Boston engineers and inspectors had been traveling to more western towns, searching for possible water supplies. They found what they were looking for in the Swift River Valley. In 1927, the state legislature passed the Swift River Act, which provided for the taking of land and the construction of the Quabbin Reservoir.

The work necessitated appropriating approximately 83,500 acres of land. The towns of Dana, Greenwich, Enfield and Prescott were totally eliminated; portions of the towns of Ware, Belchertown, Pelham, Shutesbury, New Salem, Wendell, Orange, Petersham, Barre and Hardwick were also affected. Over 136 miles of state highways were relocated and

16 miles of the Boston & Albany Railroad were abolished. Approximately 2,500 people living in 650 homes in the area were compelled to relocate. Over 7,500 bodies previously buried in 34 cemeteries were moved to newly built Quabbin Cemetery in Belchertown. By 1939 the valley was completely cleared of all traces of human habitation; the reservoir was filled by 1946.

According to Ruth Rice, a former resident of Dana, "This remarkable engineering achievement which brought life to the metropolitan Boston area cost the 2,500 residents of the valley their homes, churches, industries and other businesses. A way of life was changed for all—our relatives, our friends and our neighbors."

But the passage of time has begun to ease the loss, resentment, and anguish of the valley people. The younger generations have come to know and love the beauty of the Quabbin Reservoir and its recreational features. They are not permitted, however, to ever forget their "lost" heritage, as the material and photos in the museum rooms in the Whitaker-Clary House continue to grow each year.

The Whitaker-Clary House stands as a memorial to the towns that were lost to the Quabbin Reservoir project.

Every room is filled with furnishings, clothing, photos and memorabilia taken from that part of the Swift River Valley that is now the reservoir. Most of what is on display has been clearly identified but many other objects and photos still remain a secret— and perhaps will forever. The vast wealth of genealogical material will, hopefully, help some future researchers to unlock any remaining secrets stored in the house.

Each summer former residents, relatives, friends and neighbors gather on the wide lawn surrounding the house for a reunion. It is a time to share memories, swap stories of the good old days and help identify old photos. These photos are among the most

The Silver Lining

Although several towns were lost to the making of the Quabbin Reservoir, there was much gained as well. Recreational activities at the Quabbin Reservoir—hiking, fishing and boating (for fishermen only) are now available. And the surrounding area, known as the North Quabbin Region, is rich in natural, scenic and recreational attractions.

The area covers nine towns and, with the exception of Athol and Orange, the area's two commercial centers, the other seven (Erving, New Salem, Petersham, Phillipston, Royalston, Warwick and Wendell) still remain quiet little New England villages. Hiking, biking, hunting, fishing, canoeing, cross-country skiing and antiquing are some of the activities to be enjoyed here.

The best of small-town Americana takes place throughout the seasons—fairs, festivals, church suppers, band concerts, footraces, pumpkin-growing contests—but two special events attract visitors from near and far. The annual "Athol-to-Orange River Rat Race" is a zany event on the Millers River with more than 300 canoes, held the first Saturday in April. The "Yankee Engine-uity In Action" steam engine show and fly-in is held the last weekend in June.

For further information, write to the North Quabbin Greater Athol-Orange Chamber of Commerce, P.O. Box 157, Athol, MA 01331; or call 508-249-3849.

treasured mementos of the past, showing the people, homes, schools, churches, and workplaces of the last generation to live in the lost towns.

It is hard to look at the myriad displays depicting the beauty and serenity of these typical little New England villages without feeling pangs of remorse. Particularly poignant are the original paintings and hand drawings, the poems and other writings of the valley people that vividly express their emotions upon leaving their homes. These feelings are perhaps best summed up by Joseph W. Russell, who wrote one of the most treasured books on the subject, *A Place Called Quabbin.*

The demolitions and razings of Valley homes, houses of worship, and public buildings were—and remain—a devastating, almost unacceptable experience. There are simply no words adequate enough to describe the depth of anguish and despair suffered by Valley residents who witnessed the event. Only the passage of time can ease (but never erase) such a loss. For their sacrifice, we who, today, respect and admire the land that is known as "Quabbin," owe Valley people an enduring debt of gratitude and of understanding.

John F. Kennedy spent his first years in this nursery.

Famous Birthplaces

Some of the most interesting old houses to visit in New England are the birthplaces of notable Americans. These homes, ranging from humble dwellings to prosperous farms and country estates, are kept as memorials to honor those men and women who have distinguished themselves in one occupation or another. Each house has a unique story to tell about the celebrated person whose life began beneath its roof.

Probably the most appealing birthplaces of all are those of former presidents of the United States. As might be expected, most of these birthplaces fall into the "humble dwelling" catagory, with one president, Franklin Pierce, rumored to have been born in a log cabin (a symbol many early presidents liked to identify themselves with). He only lived there for a few weeks, however, while his family's more elegant mansion was being completed.

The birthplaces of John Adams and John Quincy Adams, located next door to each other, are both small, simple farmhouses. Both houses have been painstakingly restored, down to the minutest detail—even their clapboards were hand-hewn from nearby trees, reflecting the building materials of the late seventeenth century. The furnishings are also precise reproductions of those of the time. Although the site is now surrounded by busy roads and commercial buildings, the houses give visitors a very real sense of the Adamses' era.

A visit to Plymouth, Vermont, however, is quite a different experience. The home of Calvin Coolidge and the surrounding town appear to be virtually unchanged from their manner at the turn of the century. Coolidge's birthplace itself is the only building in town that has actually undergone renovation. Containing the original furnishings, the house has been completely restored to its state the year Coolidge was born.

The neighborhood and the house in Brookline, Massachusetts, where John Fitzgerald Kennedy was born have not changed dramatically since the Kennedy days. The street is noisier; there is more traffic; more houses have been built. But the Kennedy birthplace remains much as it was when JFK was born.

All the houses described here are, for the most part, striking in their simplicity, giving little indication of their occupant's future prominent address—1600 Pennsylvania Avenue, Washington, D.C.

Two Harvard Men

Adams Birthplaces
Quincy, Massachusetts
1681 and 1663

133 and 141
Franklin Street
Quincy, Mass.
617-773-1177

OPEN:
April 19–
November 10
Daily: 9–5

ADMISSION:
Inquire for prices.

The "Adams Birthplaces" is a most distinctive historical site. Two houses, located only 55 yards apart, are not only the two oldest presidential birthplaces in the country, but the homes of the only father and son—John Adams and John Quincy Adams—to become presidents of the United States.

The small Adams compound began in 1720, when John Adams' father, Deacon John Adams, bought a house and six acres from Joseph Penniman. It was here that the nation's second president was born and spent much of his early life.

The town (part of Braintree at that time) was very rural, and provided a haven for young boys who liked to fish, hunt and roam through the woods. Although John was small for his age, he was agile, muscular and very competitive. Early on, he perfected wrestling skills to make up for what he lacked in stature, thus developing the feisty characteristics that would stay with him throughout his life.

John, Sr., farmed the land during the growing season. In the winter he practiced the trade of cordwinding, or ropemaking. He was a devout man, a leader in his church and in the community. He instilled all of these values in his son. Young John emulated his father in all ways, even choosing farming as his life's occupation.

John, Sr., was determined to have his oldest son better himself by attending college. To discourage him from farming, he took him to the mud flats. They spent the entire day on their knees in the hot sun and thick mud, gathering bundles of thatch. At dinner that evening, the elder Adams asked his tired and aching son if he still preferred farming to going to school, and was dismayed when his son replied in the affirmative. Nevertheless, to please his father, young John went off to Harvard.

While at Harvard, John pursued the study of law, and quickly became known for his intelligence and fiery oratory. He also developed interests in history and politics, particularly concerning relations between Great Britain and the colonies. After graduation, he returned to his parents' home in Quincy, where he set up his law practice; shortly thereafter, he became enmeshed in political affairs.

John, Sr., purchased the second house on the property from Samuel Belcher in 1744. Upon the death of John, Sr., in 1761, young John inherited this second house. It was here, Penn's Hill cottage, that he brought his bride Abigail; it was also here that their second child, John Quincy Adams, was born.

While John was in Philadelphia as a delegate to the Continental Congress, Abigail was left at the house for long periods of time, tending the farm, house and children. During this time, she penned many of her famous letters. It was also in this house that John Adams, upon his return from Philadelphia, drafted the Constitution of Massachusetts.

The Adams birthplaces are now a National Historic Site.

Following this, John Adams sailed to France to negotiate and sign the Treaty of Paris, which concluded

the American Revolutionary War. Abigail and their daughter, Nabby, joined him in Paris for almost a year.

Upon their return to Braintree, they did not live in the Penn's Hill cottage again—they acquired a much larger house. The Old House, as it is still called today, is about a quarter of a mile away. Here, John Adams was preparing to finally fulfill his dream of farming; that did not come to pass. For the next 12 years, he served as vice president and president in succession to George Washington.

John Quincy Adams followed in his father's footsteps, graduating from Harvard after studying law. His education, however, was enhanced by his exten-

More Rooms for Abigail

In 1788, when John Adams purchased his "mansion house" in Quincy, it was already considered an old house. It had been built around 1731 by Major Leonard Vassall, a noted Tory who abandoned the house and property during the Revolution. Upon her return from Europe, Abigail is said to have been disappointed with the house. It was much smaller than she had remembered it, and she had become used to living in a grander style while in London at the Court of St. James.

John had expected to retire and become a farmer upon his return to Quincy, so they named the house Peacefield. But public duties, first as vice president and then as president, prevented him from doing so. Abigail, during John's absence, immediately set to work and doubled the size of the house. Peacefield became The Old House, as the family preferred to call it.

It was to this house that John Adams returned to finally retire in 1801 after his defeat for a second presidential term. He died here on July 4, 1826, on the fiftieth anniversary of the Declaration of Independence. Only a few hours before him, his old rival, Thomas Jefferson, had died at his home in Virginia.

Four generations of the Adams family continued to live in the Old House until it was bequethed to the National Park Service in 1946. For more information, call 617-773-1177.

sive overseas travels with his father. By the time he was 14 years old, John Quincy had visited Europe several times and had served as private secretary and interpreter to the American Minister to Russia in St. Petersburg. John Quincy had a long political career, which kept him away from the town of Quincy for much of his life. Following the deaths of his parents, however, he maintained both birthplaces as well as the Old House.

The Adamses continued to own the two birthplaces, renting them to tenants until 1893. It was in 1893 that the houses were first shown as museum houses by the Quincy Historical Society. They were given to the city of Quincy by the Adams family in 1940, and are now administered by the National Park Service.

The John Adams Birthplace has been restored to represent the time that his parents lived there. The furnishings are faithful reproductions of the period, made especially for the house by the Adams National Historic Site Commission.

The furnishings for the John Quincy Adams Birthplace are precise reproductions of those that were in the house when John Quincy lived there; the original pieces are still in the Old House. Expecially interesting in this house is John Adams' old law office, in which Adams, James Bowdoin and Samuel Adams drafted the Massachusetts State Constitution, which was the model for the U.S. Constitution. The original furnishings include the table on which the constitution was written and signed, as well as a bookcase filled with John Adams' books.

Franklin Pierce Homestead

Hillsborough, New Hampshire

1804

Route 31
Hillsborough, N.H.
603-464-5858

OPEN:
Memorial Day
weekend–
mid-October
Sat: 10–4
Holidays: 10–4

July–August
Fri: 10–4

ADMISSION:
Inquire for prices.

Franklin Pierce, the fourteenth president of the United States, was actually born in a log cabin, but grew up in comparitive luxury. The site of the house he was born in is now at the bottom of a reservoir, while the handsome house he actually grew up in, the elegant Pierce Homestead, still stands in the center of town and is open to the public.

Franklin's father, Benjamin Pierce, served in the Revolutionary War under General Washington. After the war, he came to the little riverside village of Hillsborough in southern New Hampshire. Through hard work as a surveyor, he was soon able to buy himself a log cabin and 50 acres of land.

A tall, handsome, distinguished-looking man with an engaging personality, Benjamin Pierce became active in the town's political affairs and was later sent to the state capitol as Hillsborough's representative. He served in many official capacities over the years, twice as the governor of New Hampshire, eventually becoming the most prominent man in the state.

It is thought that early on, just before his marriage in 1788, the log cabin was torn down and a frame house was built in its place. When his first wife died, he remarried. By the time his second wife was having their sixth child—Franklin—Benjamin, now fairly prosperous, had just completed building the house that is visited today and known as the Pierce Homestead.

Franklin was brought to the Homestead within the first few weeks of his life and spent the next 30 years there. If not his actual birthplace, it was his boyhood home and it was here that he spent his formative years under the strict guidance of his father.

Growing up under his father's strong influence,

and with much the same outgoing personality, it was natural that Franklin would pursue a political career. He was only 25 years old when he was appointed Hillsborough's representative to the state legislature (his father was now governor of the state) and, at the age of 29, he was elected to the United States Congress.

But what might have been a brilliant political career was soon to be marked by a series of misfortunes and personal tragedies. His wife, Jane Appleton, a thin and frail woman, was ill throughout most of her life. She hated politics and the Washington social scene, and constantly begged Franklin to pursue another career. The Pierces had three sons, one of whom died in infancy. Their second son died at the age of four. Their lives soon became centered around their only remaining child, Benjamin, whom they called Bennie.

In 1842, Pierce finally gave in to his wife's wishes, and resigned from his post as senator. He returned to Concord, New Hampshire, to practice law. But when the Mexican War broke out in 1846, he enlisted at once, and was promoted to brigadier-general.

Upon his return from the war, after rejecting several important government positions, he once again took up the practice of law, becoming one of the leading attorneys in New Hampshire. But his love of political life never flagged. In 1853, Pierce, at the insistence of former political colleagues, allowed his name to be put before the Democratic Convention as a candidate for president of the United States. He was the lesser of four or five more prominent candidates, and he assured his wife that he would never win. When word came that he had indeed been nominated, he was astonished. His wife promptly fainted! Several weeks after Pierce was elected president, Jane Pierce began to reconcile herself to the inevitable and made preparations for the move to Washington.

In January, just before the inauguration, while the Pierces were returning to Concord from a short trip to Boston, the train they were riding on went off the track and rolled down an embankment. The wooden car broke apart. Franklin and Jane were uninjured, but their beloved son, Bennie, suffered a severe blow to the head and was killed instantly.

Jane Pierce never recovered from this tragedy. She was too overcome with grief to attend the inauguration. When she finally returned to Washington many months later, she rarely engaged in social activities. She was referred to by the press as "the shadow in the White House."

Franklin performed his duties with a heavy heart. His four-year administration was not considered successful or significant by most historians. His support of the Compromise of 1850, which attempted to give each state the right to decide about the slavery issue, made him very unpopular with abolitionist friends at home. Later, his declaration that the Emancipation Proclamation was unconstitutional sealed his fate, particularly in New England, where the seeds of abolition first took hold.

After his wife died in 1863, Pierce spent the remaining years of his life in political obscurity. He had become so unpopular in his home state that it was more than 50 years after his death before a statue was erected in his honor.

Today, the small village of Hillsborough, New Hampshire, which has remained much as it was during Franklin's boyhood, takes great pride in the restoration of this elegant homestead. It contains many mementos of the fourteenth president of the United States and his family. It is operated by the New Hampshire Division of Parks and maintained by the Hillsborough Historical Society.

Rescued by the Pierce Brigade

The house that Franklin Pierce owned and occupied when he lived in Concord, New Hampshire, was saved from demolition in 1971 by a specially formed group called The Pierce Brigade. It was moved to its present site in Concord's Historic District and given the name "manse," (an early term for "the dwelling of a landholder") to distinguish it from Pierce's birthplace.

Pierce and his family lived here from 1842 to 1848, during the period when he came to Concord to establish a law firm. Shortly after moving into the house, the Pierce's oldest son, four-year-old Franky, died of typhus. Pierce left the house in 1846 to go off to the Mexican War, while his wife and little Benny went to stay with relatives. It is thought that he never wished to return to the house—its rooms for him were haunted by the memory of Franky's death. A unique portrait of Franky by a local artist is one of the treasures in The Manse.

The modified Greek design of the house is similar to many houses of that period in Concord. It has been completely restored to duplicate the way it looked when the Pierces lived there. Many of the current furnishings belonged to Franklin Pierce and other members of his family; some pieces are known as "White House Pieces" (including the president's inaugural top hat). Call 603-224-9620 for more information.

The House on Beals Street

John Fitzgerald Kennedy National Historic Site
Brookline, Massachusetts
1 9 0 9

83 Beals Street
Brookline, Mass.
617-566-7937

OPEN:
Daily 10–4:30
Personal guided
tours by National
Park Rangers at
10:30 and 11:45, and
from 1–4 on the
hour. Portions of
audiotape narrative
available by special
request.

ADMISSION:
Inquire for prices.

Visitors to the John F. Kennedy birthplace are guaranteed a unique experience—their "tour" through this home is accompanied by the voice of Rose Kennedy, the mother of the thirty-fifth president of the United States. Each room in this modest two-story home in suburban Boston has a small button on the wall. When pushed, the voice of Rose describes the happy, early years of her marriage.

Particularly poignant is her description of the master bedroom. In the twin bed closest to the window ("where the light would be best for the doctor") her second son, John Fitzgerald, was born. Mrs. Kennedy describes her feelings at the birth: "When you hold your baby in your arms the first time, and you think of all the things you can say and do to influence him, it's a tremendous responsibility. What you do with him and for him can influence not only him, but everyone he meets—and not for a day or a month or a year, but for time and for eternity."

She adds, "Later, when Jack was elected president, I thought how fortunate I was out of all the millions of mothers in the United States to be the one to have her son inaugurated president on that cold, cold day."

The nursery where Jack spent his first four years is dominated by a large bassinet, used by Kennedy children and grandchildren. "We spent a lot of time reading and entertaining the children here in this room, particularly when Jack had scarlet fever in 1920," says Mrs. Kennedy.

Toys are strewn about the room and a small bookcase holds books, Jack's "favorite pastime." Visitors hear Mrs. Kennedy tell of his love for adventure books, especially *King Arthur and His Knights*.

Rose Kennedy used a small room off the master bedroom for her study. A devoted mother, she describes the card file on top of her desk in which she faithfully recorded the important health information of her children—height, weight, diet, vaccinations.

Other rooms, moderate in size, include the dining room where formal meals were held at a large table (a little table was set with sterling silver bowls and utensils for the children) and an old-fashioned kitchen with a large black stove. The stove was in almost constant use, according to Mrs. Kennedy, with "baby bottles to be sterilized, formulas to prepare and meals to cook."

When the Kennedys lived in this house at 83 Beals Street, the neighborhood was much less populated. Surrounding vacant lots gave the feeling of openness. As visitors depart through the back door they are left with a parting thought from Rose Kennedy. She often stood here, looking out at her children laughing and playing in the backyard.

The nursery at 83 Beals Street.

"We were very happy here. And although we did not know about the days ahead, we were enthusiastic and optimistic about the future."

John lived in this house until he was four years old. After the birth of his sisters, Rosemary and Kathleen, the family moved to a lrger house a short distance away. The Edward Devotion School, which John attended, and St. Aiden's, the church where he was baptized, still stand in the neighborhood. The Dexter School, which John also attended, has since changed location. But it was here, according to Rose Kennedy, that John developed a love for learning and sports.

John graduated from Harvard and entered the Navy, serving heroically in World War II. On his return to Boston, he embarked on his political career—he was elected to the House of Representatives in 1946. He moved into his seat in Congress in 1952, and was elected president just eight years later.

The Library on the Point

Sharing space on Columbia Point in Boston Harbor with the Boston campus of the University of Massachusetts, the John F. Kennedy Library looms up from the tip of of the point, commanding a majestic view of the harbor and the city. The nine-story, concrete, steel and glass building was designed by I. M. Pei.

While the library itself is busy every day with researchers, most people come here to see the museum and the exhibits of Kennedy memorabilia. A visit here begins in the theater with an introductory film about the President, his life and times. From there you enter the large, circular museum room. Here, through the use of large photographs and displays of personal mementos, you follow a timeline of the Kennedy family, highlighted with the sights and sounds of major national and international events during "the Kennedy years."

An exact replica of the desk from the Oval Office (with copies of some of the President's "doodles" sitting on top of it), Kennedy's famous rocking chair and many reminders of his inauguration are all part of the displays. For more information, call 617-929-4523.

A Vermont Boyhood

Route 100A (6 miles
south of U.S. 4)
Plymouth Notch,
Vermont
802-828-3226

OPEN:
Late May–
mid-October
Daily: 9:30–5:30

ADMISSION:
Inquire for prices.

The Calvin Coolidge Birthplace

Plymouth Notch, Vermont

1 8 4 0

It is still possible when visiting the rural Vermont village of Plymouth Notch to get a true sense of what life was like when the thirtieth president of the United States, Calvin Coolidge, was born here on the 4th of July, 1872. This entire hamlet, now a National Historic District, is considered to be the best preserved presidential birthplace in the nation.

Virtually unchanged since the turn of the century, the homes of the Coolidge family and neighbors, the general store, the community church, the one-room schoolhouse, the post office and the Plymouth Cheese Factory still stand and most have their original furnishings. The cheese factory, built in 1890 by Coolidge's grandfather, is now owned by Calvin's oldest son, John. It still produces cheese (made from the original recipe), which can be purchased on the site.

The General Store, formerly owned and operated by Calvin's father, is also still in operation. Attached to the rear of the building is the simple, unpretentious living quarters where the family lived—a five-room, 1½-story cottage, with unpainted, narrow clapboards and small windows. It was here that Calvin Coolidge was born.

When Calvin was four years old, shortly after the birth of his only other sibling, Abigail, the family moved across the street to a more spacious house. Here Calvin was responsible for filling the wood box and caring for the animals. He was clever with his hands, as is evidenced by a quilt he made when he was ten years old. A miniature chest of drawers that he made is also displayed in a downstairs bedroom. The quilt, made in the "tumbling blocks" pattern, is of a particularly challenging design.

As he grew older, he assumed many typical farm duties, including plowing, planting, haying and harvesting. His favorite job was "sugaring." He also enjoyed tagging along with his father, "Colonel John," on his official duties as the local constable and deputy sheriff.

This peaceful, isolated village in the heart of the Green Mountains was, in Calvin Coolidge's words, "a fine atmosphere in which to raise a boy . . . there was little about it that was artificial . . . even when I try to divest it of the halo which I know always surrounds the past, I am unable to create any other impression than that it was fresh and clean."

The greatest significance attached to Plymouth Notch, and the Coolidge Homestead in particular, occurred here in 1923. Coolidge, then vice president of the United States, was vacationing here that summer when he received word of the unexpected death of President Warren G. Harding.

"On the night of August 2, 1923, I was awakened by my father coming up the stairs calling my name," wrote Coolidge in his autobiography. "I noticed that

This general store is attached to the birthplace of Calvin Coolidge.

his voice trembled. As the only times I had ever observed that before were when death had visited our family, I knew that something of the gravest nature had occurred."

His father, who had just been awakened by the delivery of a telegram, addressed his son as "Mr. Presi-

---

Silent Cal

Calvin Coolidge was a man of few words; he had little use for small talk or social banter. His quick wit and dry sense of humor, however, combined with his nasal twang, made him a hit with reporters. By the time he retired from public office, he left behind a string of anecdotes that endeared him to the American people. Here are a few:

One night at a Washington dinner party, a society matron sitting next to him said, "Mr. President, I just made a bet with a friend that I could get you to say more than two words."

"You lose," retorted the president.

After finishing a speech at Madison Square Garden one day, a woman approached the president and gushed, "Mr. President, I enjoyed your speech so much that I stood up the whole time!"

"So did I," Coolidge replied.

One Sunday when Coolige returned from church, his wife asked him what the preacher had talked about.

"Sin," replied Mr. Coolidge.

"What did the preacher say about it?" pressed Mrs. Coolidge.

"He was against it," said the president.

While Coolidge was presiding over the state senate in Boston one day, a heated argument arose between two members and terminated with one of the legislators telling the other to "go to hell."

The offended senator appealed to Coolidge and demanded that something be done.

Without changing his expression or composure, Coolidge replied:

"I have looked up the rules; you don't have to go."

dent," and told him of Harding's death. Coolidge and his wife arose and dressed quickly. The elder Coolidge, who held the office of notary public, was able to administer the presidential oath of office to his son.

The simple ceremony was held at 2:47 A.M. in the sitting room of the house by the light of a kerosene lamp and with the family Bible close at hand. (According to Coolidge it was not officially used "as it is not the practice in Vermont and Massachusetts to use a Bible in connection with the administration of an oath.")

Only a few local people, the vice president's wife, his young assistant secretary and his chauffeur were in attendance as the elder Coolidge read the oath in its entirety and Calvin repeated it without hesitation.

The Coolidges left for Washington later that day, but were to return to this peaceful haven often. When Calvin Coolidge died in 1933, his body was returned for burial in the nearby cemetery where six generations of his family had been laid to rest. His gravesite is marked with an unpretentious stone, much like the ones surrounding it. The only thing that distinguishes it from the others is the Presidential Seal of the United States that appears above his name.

Prudence Crandall, the founder of New England's first black female academy.

History-Making Houses

Of the more than 600 houses throughout New England that have been carefully preserved and are open to the public, approximately three-quarters of them are listed in the National Register of Historic Places. Many are also officially registered as National Historic Landmarks. Some of these houses are among the oldest in the country; some were the scene of important activities relating to both the Revolutionary and Civil wars; some tell stories of important landmarks in black history and famous American figures. Included here are a few houses, less well known then those inhabited by great statesmen, presidents and the like, but some that have nevertheless played a part in shaping the history of our country.

The Webb-Deane-Stevens Museum

Wethersfield, Connecticut
1752; 1766; 1788

203–215 Main Street
Wethersfield, Conn.
203-529-6012

OPEN:
March–December
Tues–Sat: 10–4
January–February
Fri–Sat: 10–4
Sun: 1–4
May 15–October 15
Sun: 1–4
Closed holidays

ADMISSION:
Inquire for prices.

The Webb-Deane-Stevens Museum is a complex of three authentically and meticulously restored eighteenth-century houses in Wethersfield, Connecticut. They are owned and operated by the National Society of the Colonial Dames of America in the State of Connecticut, one of the earliest preservation groups in the state. The three houses have been carefully restored and painstakingly furnished to reflect the lifestyles of their inhabitants—the families of a merchant, a diplomat and a tradesman.

Wethersfield was once called Oniontown, due to the famous "Wethersfield Red" onions grown here and shipped to the West Indies and parts of Europe. By the early 1800s, well over a million bunches of onions a year were shipped far and wide, and their aromatic smell gave Wethersfield a rather notorious reputation.

Like so many other small towns that grew up along the Connecticut River in the eighteenth century, Wethersfield's economy relied heavily on trade with the West Indies. Wethersfield was one of the most important river ports along the way. Successful merchants owned their own ships and built fine homes in town.

One such merchant was Joseph Webb, whose sailing vessels traveled and traded throughout the West Indies. He built the Webb House for his family in 1752, but died in 1761 (at age 34), leaving a wife and six children. When Mrs. Webb married Silas Deane, her lawyer, two years later, he built her a new home next door (see the Deane House, on page 168). Her two older children, Joseph, Jr., and Samuel, lived on in their father's house, and Joseph, Jr., continued his father's business as well. During the Revolutionary

War, he became active in supplying clothing and food to the Continental Army. He later married Abigail Chester, who was such a delightful hostess—bringing great fame to the house with her important guests—that the house was soon nicknamed Hospitality Hall.

In 1781, one of the most important and decisive meetings of the Revolutionary War was held in the Webb House. The war had not been going well for the patriots, and Washington's armies were bogged down north of New York City. The French army, under the command of the Count de Rochambeau, had come to a similar stalemate in Newport, Rhode Island. General Washington and Count de Rochambeau met at the Webb house for a four-day conference and decided to combine their forces. The two commanders marched their troops south and, in October 1781, the combined armies defeated the British at Yorktown. This proved to be the last major battle of the war.

The parlor of the two-story gambrel-roofed frame house where Washington met with Rochambeau has the dignified look of a room where such important

The lives of three eighteenth-century families are reflected at the Webb-Deane-Stevens Museum.

decisions could easily be made. It is decorated with furniture handsomely crafted in the mid-eighteenth century by Wethersfield cabinetmakers and chair-makers. The bedroom, one of the few documented places where Washington *really* slept, still has the original red-flocked wallpaper hung in honor of his visit. Many of the original pieces of furniture built by local craftsmen and several portraits owned by the Webb family are on display, along with some fine examples of handmade quilts, coverlets and bedclothes.

Just next door to the Webb House and closely associated with it is the Silas Deane House. The first question a docent will ask you as you begin a tour of this house is, "What do you know about Silas Deane?" Without waiting for a snide answer alluding to Deane's notoriety as a traitor, she will quickly state, "He was a *much* maligned man!"

Deane, the son of a blacksmith, went to Yale to study law. Shortly after being admitted to the bar in 1761 he began a practice in Wethersfield and became the legal advisor to the wealthy widow Mehitable Webb (see the Webb House, above). Two years later he married her and built her this grand house next to the Webbs'.

Deane's interest in politics led him to become a delegate to the First Continental Congress, where he was commisioned in 1776 to travel abroad to develop Franco-American trade. Ambitious and arrogant, he made political enemies who accused him of misappropriation of public funds. He was recalled by Congress and branded a traitor after some of his personal letters were made public.

Deane valiantly fought throughout his remaining years to clear his name, but died abroad in poverty and disgrace. It wasn't until 50 years later, in 1842, that Congress finally absolved him of all wrongdoing by charging his auditors with "gross injustice" and granting his heirs $37,000 as restitution.

The Deane house, built in 1766, is elegantly furnished with fine examples of Queen Anne and Chippendale period pieces, rare china, antique silver and colorful bed and window treatments. Visitors are welcomed into an unusually spacious front hallway with an elaborate staircase. The big country kitchen with its many authentic utensils on display also has an interesting brass clock jack that controls a spit in the large fireplace. Dried herbs collected from the gardens out behind the house hang in the kitchen. Weather permitting, you can wander through the herb and flower gardens. The dining room table has been set for a meal, carefully illustrating the lifestyle of the family that lived here.

The third house in this museum was built by Isaac Stevens in 1788, and remained in the same family for 170 years. Stevens was a leather tanner and saddler by trade. This house illustrates the lifestyle of a more

---

The Most Ancient Town in Connecticut

The Webb-Deane-Stevens Museum is in the heart of Wethersfield's Historic District—the largest in Connecticut. There are more than 150 structures built before 1850 still standing in "the most ancient town in Connecticut," and all of them still stand on their original ground. A dozen or more of the buildings are open to the public on a regular basis; others are open on special occasions.

The Buttolph-Williams House is a turn-of-the-century "mansion house" built in the English Tudor style, and is particularly interesting to visit. It has a fine collection of period furnishings; of special note is the large kitchen said to be the most authentic and completely furnished of its type in New England. For information call 203-529-0460.

The Wethersfield Historical Society, 150 Main Street, is located in the Old Academy Museum. It houses a large collection of local history, maritime lore, genealogy, tools, crafts, furniture and decorative arts, and maintains several other historical buildings. Call the society at 203-529-7656 for information.

The Comstock, Ferre & Co., 223 Main Street, founded in 1820, is the oldest continuously operating seed company in the country. It occupies a collection of old buildings and some of its more than 850 varieties of vegetable, flower and herb seeds are kept in antique seed bins. For information call 203-529-3319.

modest household of the period (compared to the Webb and Deane houses), and gives some insight into the everyday activities of an ordinary family of the times.

The Stevens House differs noticeably from its companion dwellings. The original wide pine floorboards, interior paneling, sliding shutters and the metal door to the brick oven in the kitchen set this house apart from the other, more elaborate, dwellings.

The Colonial Dames have used the second floor of the house to display some unusual collections—a closet full of women's dainty white head coverings; examples of nineteenth-century needlework; and a wonderful room full of toys, games and dolls of the nineteenth century. Many of the furnishings of the house were owned by the Stevens family and represent the accumulation of several generations of family inhabitants.

A School For Young Ladies and Misses of Color

Prudence Crandall House

Canterbury, Connecticut
1805

Canterbury Green
Canterbury, Conn.
203-546-9916

OPEN:
January 15–
December 15
Wed–Sun: 1–4:30

ADMISSION:
Inquire for prices.

Prudence Crandall, a small, slightly built young woman with large dark eyes and a warm smile, had an engaging and energetic personality. As the eldest daughter in a prosperous farming family, she enjoyed a happy childhood and grew up wanting to be a teacher. When she was 16 years old, her Quaker parents, believing that girls should be educated as well as boys, sent her to a boarding school in Providence.

Upon graduating, she taught at a school in the nearby town of Plainfield. She was so successful as a teacher—and so popular with her students—that a group of citizens from her hometown of Canterbury asked her to come there and open a school for their daughters. She purchased a large house in the center of town and began her school in the fall of 1831.

All went well until the following year, when Prudence admitted a young Negro girl, Sarah Harris, the daughter of a respectable farmer, to the school. When parents of the white girls threatened to withdraw their children unless Prudence "sent the nigger away," she held firm and refused to do so.

In order to ensure that she would have enough students to keep the school open the following fall, Prudence advertised for "young ladies and misses of color" to board at her school. Thus, the first black female academy in New England was established.

The townspeople reacted in anger, unanimously denouncing her school at a town meeting. Her students were harassed and her school was nearly burned down. Prudence was arrested and jailed for breaking the infamous, hastily passed Connecticut "Black Law," which made it illegal to establish any school or academy for the instruction of "colored persons who are not inhabitants of this State."

She was released from jail on a technicality and re-opened the school. Shortly afterward, the school was stormed by a group of enraged citizens. They smashed windows and doors, demolished the furniture and polluted the well. Fearing for the safety of the girls, Prudence regretfully decided to close the school and leave town.

Although this ended Connecticut's first educational experiment in desegregation, the incident is said to have advanced the status of blacks, and to help bring a quicker end to slavery in Connecticut. In 1886, the Connecticut legislature "did penance for the state's earlier policy" by voting a small pension for Prudence Crandall as recompence for her losses.

Prudence's beautiful white Georgian-style house with its fine architectural detail has been carefully restored by the Connecticut Historical Commission. The three main rooms on the first floor are filled with both permanent and changing exhibits on the life of Prudence Crandall and her school, the story of black people in pre–Civil War Connecticut, and eighteenth- and nineteenth-century local history.

This stately home stands as a monument to Prudence Crandall and her students.

Growing Up Green

The northeast corner of Connecticut—no longer the scene of rebellious times as those known by Prudence Crandall, Nathan Hale and Israel Putnam—is now called "Connecticut's Quiet Corner." It still retains the rural flavor of earlier days, with its rolling hillsides dotted with farms and small villages. Gardening and farming on a professional and personal level are important here and the products from some of the local farms and greenhouses have become internationally known.

For the gardening buff, here are a few places of special note to visit while in the area: Buell's Greenhouses, Inc. (203-974-0623) in Eastford is internationally known in the horticultural world for its hybrid gloxinias. Logee's Greenhouse (203-774-8083) in Danielson is the oldest horticultural business in Connecticut and has been continuously operated by the same family since 1892; it has the largest begonia collection in the east. Select Seeds (203-684-5655) in Union specializes in seeds, plants and information on authentic old-fashioned period gardens (its customers include gardeners from Old Sturbridge Village, Mount Vernon and Monticello). Caprilands Herb Farm (203-742-7244) in Coventry has 38 herb gardens, several shops and an eighteenth-century house open to gardening groups for lunches and teas.

The Woodstock Fair, a typical New England fair with food, animals, exhibits and entertainment, is a major event in this area. It has been held annually for more than 130 years and draws record-breaking crowds (usually on Labor Day weekend). Call 203-774-3246 for information.

Brother Jonathan

West Town Street,
(at the junction of
Routes 87 and 207)
Lebanon, Conn.
203-642-7558

OPEN:
May 15–October 15
Tues–Sat: 1–5
Sun: by
appointment

ADMISSION:
Donation requested.

The Jonathan Trumbull House

Lebanon, Connecticut

1 7 3 5

The exterior of the solidly built Jonathan Trumbull House in the small village of Lebanon, Connecticut, has an overall peaceful, stately look. It gives no hint of the feverish, clandestine activities that surrounded it in 1776. Once inside, however, particularly in Governor Trumbull's windowless second-floor bedroom with its well-concealed escape passage and sentry box (where a guard once stood duty day and night), you get a sense of the intrigue and conspiracy that took place here during the Revolutionary War.

The house was built for Jonathan and his wife by his father, Joseph Trumbull, a merchant shipowner. Upon graduating from Harvard, Jonathan returned to Lebanon to assist his father in his mercantile business, the largest and most prosperous in the colonies.

At the age of 23, having proven himself a successful businessman, he was elected to the General Assembly of Connecticut. He subsequently held every public office in the state. He was governor for more than 14 years before, during and after the Revolutionary War.

The Trumbull house was located on Post Road, the most direct thoroughfare between New York and Boston. This made the town of Lebanon an important communications center between New England and the southern colonies at the time of the Revolutionary War. Behind the house, a small building—the "War Office"—served as the transfer center for goods and arms. Merchandise was brought here from ships anchored in Norwich and Haddam. Supplies for the Continental Army—arms, tents, food and clothing—were loaded onto carts for delivery.

An underground tunnel was built between the "office" and the house so that the governor, who held important meetings here with many famous patriots, could pass to and from the building without being seen. A price was set on his head by the British because of his support of the colonies. So important was his contribution to the war effort that George Washington noted in his diary, "Except for Brother Jonathan, the war could not have been carried to a successful conclusion." The term "Brother Jonathan" thus became another name for a patriotic American.

The house is now owned and operated by the Connecticut Daughters of the American Revolution and contains many original Trumbull possessions. Visitors can see items such as an early Queen Anne chair used by the governor in his pew at church, and his old, well-worn broad-brimmed hat.

Adjacent to the house is the historic Wadsworth Stable where George Washington kept his favorite horse, Nelson, during his frequent visits to Connecticut. The stable was originally located in Hartford, but moved to its present location in 1954. Now it is the repository for an interesting collection of Revolutionary War items such as ox-carts, wagons and iron ware. The war office is still standing, and is open to visitors on Saturdays during the summer.

The Trumbull House, quiet now, was full of clandestine activity during the Revolutionary War.

Digestive History

Situated on the same property and just behind the Governor Trumbull House is another historic house that was moved to this site in 1974. It is the birthplace and boyhood home of Dr. William Beaumont, the "Father of Gastric Physiology."

Shortly after serving in the War of 1812, Dr. Beaumont was assigned to a wildlife frontier post, Fort Mackinac in northern Michigan. While Beaumont was on duty there, a young French Canadian fur trapper was brought into his office, near death from a gunshot wound to the left lower chest and stomach. Beaumont was able to save the young man's life, but all efforts to close the wound failed, leaving a gaping hole in the patient's stomach.

Beaumont was able to keep the young man under observation off and on for the next 11 years. During this time he made a series of remarkable studies on gastric secretion, the first ever made on a living person. His studies, conducted under primitive conditions, culminated in his now classic *Experiments and Observations on the Gastric Juice and the Physiology of Digestion,* published in 1833. It was widely acclaimed and published in many countries. Beaumont has been memorialized by many medical organizations and buildings that bear his name.

In 1970, members of the Beaumont Medical Club of Yale University School of Medicine purchased his birthplace, restored it and opened it to the public. The house contains a re-creation of an early nineteenth-century doctor's examination room, complete with antique medical instruments typical of the period. For information call 203-642-7247.

Mumbet's Revolt

Colonel John Ashley House

Ashley Falls, Massachusetts
1735

The Ashley House is one of the oldest and finest examples of Colonial architecture in western Massachusetts. It was built in 1735 by Colonel John Ashley. His father had come out to the wilderness from Boston in 1722, bought land from the Indians and established two townships—Ashley Falls and Sheffield.

John Ashley became a leading citizen of the town, held positions as selectman and moderator of Sheffield, served several terms in the General Court in Boston and a long tenure as judge of the Court of Common Pleas. He was a colonel in the army in the French and Indian War, and furnished iron and supplies during the American Revolution.

His house was often the scene of political gatherings. Two events that occurred in the house were of particular significance, affecting the course of regional and state history. In 1773, an 11-man committee met in Colonel Ashley's study to draw up the Sheffield Declaration of Independence, a statement of grievances against English rule. It clearly stated that all people were "equal, free and independent." The Declaration was adopted at the town meeting on January 12, 1773. Called "America's first declaration of independence from England," it predated the United States Constitution by three years.

The second important historical event to take place in the Ashley House was a direct result of the first. Mrs. Ashley's black slave, Mumbet (her real name was Florence Freeman), overhearing the talk at this and other meetings at the house, became aware of the possibilities for her own freedom. One night, after a bitter argument with Mrs. Ashley, Mumbet ran away to the home of the Sedgwick family. She pleaded with Mr. Sedgwick, a lawyer, to file a suit for her on the

Copper Hill Road
Ashley Falls, Mass.
413-229-8600

OPEN:
May 25–October 14
Wed–Sun: 1–5
Open most
holidays.

ADMISSION:
Inquire for prices.

basis of the new constitutional clause declaring that all people were born free and equal.

Theodore Sedgwick, although a close personal friend of Colonel Ashley, felt Mumbet was right. With Tapping Reeve as associate council, he brought the case to court and won Mumbet's freedom. Colonel Ashley decided not to appeal the case and, in so doing, was the first in Massachusetts to recognize abolition by the new state constitution.

Mumbet stayed with the Sedgwicks and worked for them as a free woman for the rest of her life. When she died, she was buried in the Sedgwick family plot in Stockbridge. Her touching epitaph was written by Catharine Maria Sedgwick, Theodore's daughter, who was particularly close to Mumbet.

Her supposed age was 85 years. She was born a slave and remained a slave for nearly 30 years. She could neither read nor write yet in her own sphere she had no superior nor equal. She neither wasted time nor property. She never violated a trust nor failed to perform a duty. In every situation of domestic trial, she was the most efficient helper, and the tenderest friend. Good Mother, farewell.

The Trustees of Reservations

The Colonel John Ashley House is one of a number of properties in the Berkshires maintained by The Trustees of Reservations (TTOR). This organization was formed in 1891 and empowered by the commonwealth of Massachusetts to hold and maintain (tax free) for the public, under suitable rules and regulations, "beautiful and historical places and tracts of land within this Commonwealth."

One of these properties is adjacent to the Ashley House. A trail leads to Bartholomew's Cobble, a marble and quartzite outcropping bordering the Housatonic River. It is considered one of the nation's most outstanding concentrations of native flora. Guides give visitors a tour of the on-site museum, and there is a picnic area available.

There are also three outstanding houses in nearby towns that are well worth a visit. The William Cullen Bryant Homestead in Cummington is the boyhood home and later summer residence of the poet and journalist. Naumkeag, near Stockbridge, is the summer home of Joseph Hodges Choate, U.S. Ambassador to the Court of St. James at the end of the reign of Queen Victoria. The Mission House in Stockbridge was built in 1739 for The Reverend John Sargeant, the first missionary to the Stockbridge Indians. A guide to these and other properties maintained by TTOR is available by writing to TTOR, 224 Adams Street, Milton, MA 02186; or call 617-698-2066.

The Underground Railroad

527 Washington
Street
Newton, Mass.
617-552-7238

OPEN:
October–June
Mon–Fri: 10–4
First Sunday: 2–5

July–August
Mon–Thu: 1–4

September
Mon–Fri: 10–4
Sun: 2–5
Thu: 1–5

ADMISSION:
Inquire for prices.

The Jackson Homestead

Newton, Massachusetts

1809

As early as 1786, but particularly from 1830 to 1861, an important section of the Underground Railroad stretched through the New England states into Canada. This loosely organized system of stations and transportation routes for fugitive slaves, which began in the southern slave-holding states, was supported by many dedicated northern abolitionists and sympathizers committed to helping slaves escape to freedom.

All along the route fugitives were secreted in private homes, barns and churches. Cellar holes, attic eaves, hidden wall panels, earthen tunnels—any small concealing space that could be found in a sympathizer's home was put to use to hide the fugitives from their masters or from bounty hunters.

The Fugitive Slave Law of 1850, although almost ignored by northerners, resulted in heavy penalties for anyone found guilty of harboring a runaway slave. Therefore, the entire operation was conducted in secrecy. Although most people knew of the existence of the Underground Railroad, few knew the names of the people involved or the location of the various hiding places.

The history of the Underground Railroad has been difficult to trace, as few records were kept of its clandestine activities. Throughout New England, houses with such hiding places are still being discovered, as alterations to old houses and remodeling of barns reveal surprising secrets of the past.

One such house in Newton, Massachusetts, is the Jackson Homestead, an important link in the Underground Railroad. William Jackson, chairman of the Board of Selectmen of Newton and deacon of the Eliot Church, was a staunch abolitionist. He was also

a member of the Boston Vigilance Committee, which, in the 1850s, raised money to assist escaped slaves. They transported slaves to Canada, helped with their medical and legal fees and provided them with clothing and spending money. Not everyone knew at that time, however, that Jackson's home in Newton was also used to *hide* runaway slaves.

William Jackson's home was an important link in the Underground Railroad.

Jackson's family was well aware of his secret activities. His daughter, Ellen, kept a journal, and often recorded events that involved aiding and hiding runaway slaves. In 1874 she wrote:

One night between twelve and one o'clock, I well remember father was awakened by pebbles thrown against his window. He rose [and] asked what was wanted? Mr. Bowditch replied it was he with a runaway slave whom he wished to hide till morning, and then help him on his way to Canada for his master was in Boston looking for him. Father took him in and next morning carried him fifteen miles to a Station where he could take a car for Canada. He could not have safely left by any Boston station.

Ellen was also president of the Freedmen's Aid Society from its formation until just before her death (a span of almost 50 years). She further relates in her journal accounts of the ladies' sewing circle that met at the homestead to sew clothes for the destitute slaves. Her account book lists the barrels of clothing, new and used, and bedding that her small group of about a dozen women shipped monthly to such destinations as Selma, Alabama; Macon, Georgia; Hampton, Virginia; and Tuskegee, Alabama. The latter shipments of clothing and bedding went directly to Booker T. Washington, founder of Tuskegee Institute—which was to become the leading black educational institution in America.

Under Ellen's leadership, her small group was also able to raise funds for several projects, including sup-

---

The Black Heritage Trail

Like the Jackson House in Newton, many houses on the northern slope of Beacon Hill in Boston provided a refuge for runaway slaves. Today, this area contains the nation's largest collection of historical sites associated with a pre–Civil War black community. The Black Heritage Trail begins at the Afro-American Museum (46 Joy Street), where you can obtain a brochure and detailed map of the area. This building is the former Abiel Smith School, the first school in the city for black children.

Just down the street is The African Meeting House (Smith Court), which was the center of the old community. It was built in 1806 for persons of African decent "who refused to continue to sit in the galleries of the white churches." It was here that William Lloyd Garrison founded the New England Anti-Slavery Society in 1832.

Several houses along Pinckney and Phillips streets were homes of abolitionists and important stops on the Underground Railroad. And not far away on the Boston Common, facing the State House, is the famous Robert Gould Shaw and 54th Regiment Memorial, a bas-relief by Augustus Saint-Gaudens. It commemorates the 54th Regiment, the first black division from the North who fought in the Civil War, and their white leader. Call 617-742-5415 for information.

port for teachers of slaves in various locations. One note in her ledger mentions that they sent funds "to Rev. G. Rowe, Charleston, to help repair his house shaken to pieces by earthquake."

One whole section of the basement in the Jackson Homestead is devoted to the history of the Underground Railroad. There is an extensive ongoing exhibit with posters, photos, books and writings about the activities of the local abolitionist movement. Two items that hold great interest to visitors, particularly schoolchildren, are reproductions of a slave collar (which can be tried on) and a large box in which Henry "Box" Brown mailed himself to freedom. Visitors can also see the deep root cellar where slaves were hidden during an emergency.

In 1887, 32 years after the death of William Jackson, the Eliot Church of Newton suffered a severe fire. When the cornerstone was unearthed, in it was found a prophecy written by William Jackson. It stated that "before this seal is broken, the sin of slavery shall be removed from this land." In that vein, the Jackson Homestead continues to foster racial harmony through a series of multicultural programs, exhibits and special educational programs for schoolchildren.

The Enigmatic Mr. Twilight

Brownington
Village Historic
District
Brownington, Vt.
802-754-2022

OPEN:
May 15–June 30
Fri–Tue: 11–5

July–August
Daily: 11–5

September 1–
October 15
Fri–Tue: 11–5

ADMISSION:
Inquire for prices.

Old Stone House

Brownington, Vermont
1 8 3 6

The Reverend Alexander Lucius Twilight, a prominent member of his community, was a man of mystery. Since his death in 1857, he has remained so in the history of the small hamlet of Brownington, Vermont. What makes this enigmatic, shadowy figure particularly intriguing is the incredible monument he left behind and the stories surrounding the construction of the Old Stone House.

Originally built as a dormitory, the Old Stone House is a massive four-story building made of large granite blocks quarried from nearby fields. It contains 30 rooms and 15 tiny charcoal-burning fireplaces, which supplied heat for the students. But what is so astounding about this great building is the fact that it was built entirely by Mr. Twilight himself.

Twilight, the son of a poor farmer, was born in 1795 in Corinth, Vermont. It is believed that his parents were either black or mulatto (records tell conflicting facts on his race), and at an early age he was indentured to a neighboring farmer. He obviously worked hard to better himself and, upon completion of his indenture, attended Randolph Academy and Middlebury College.

Middlebury College claims Alexander Twilight as the first black American college graduate (class of 1823), thus giving rise to the mystery of whether he was actually a black man. (He was often described by contemporaries as "swarthy.") Both Amherst and Bowdoin, which gave degrees to black students in 1826, dispute Middlebury's claim.

Later, Twilight was elected to the Vermont state legislature for a two-year term. Once again, he was claimed as the first black American legislator—and once again, the claim is still under doubt.

After graduating from college, Twilight taught in several schools and was licensed to preach. He came to Brownington in 1829 with his new wife to serve as minister of the Congregational Church and as principal of the Orleans County Grammar School—also known as Brownington Academy, the only secondary school in the county.

Under his leadership, the academy became very popular and student enrollment rose significantly. Finding places for boarding students to live, however, soon became a problem. Twilight petitioned the Board of Trustees to build a dormitory for them. When they refused, he decided to build one himself. No one knows how he acquired the funds to do so on his meager salary, but he not only found the money, he actually built the building almost entirely by himself.

His building methods were extraordinary—it is believed that he used a wooden or earthen staging that rose as the building rose. An ox, turning a treadmill on the platform, lifted each handmade stone into place and, as the building rose, so did the ox and the

The Old Stone House, built entirely by the Reverend Alexander Lucius Twilight.

treadmill. Legend has it that when the last stone was laid in place at the top of the building, there was no way to safely bring the ox back down—so it was slaughtered on the staging and used to provide a great feast in celebration of the completed building.

The four-story building, which Twilight christened "Athenian Hall" in veneration of ancient Greek scholars, has walls that are 20 inches thick. The first floor contained a music room, an enormous kitchen with a huge fireplace and a large dining room. The second and third floors were divided into 20 student rooms, and the fourth floor was used as an assembly hall.

Although the handsome new dormitory lacked indoor plumbing or central heating, students flocked to the school, paying $1.50 per term for room and board. Lessons ranged from 50 cents (for vocal music) to

Twilight's Town

Almost the entire village of Brownington, dominated by the Old Stone House, is incorporated into a historic district. The Orleans County Historical Society manages several of the properties, including the Old Stone House Museum, the Twilight Homestead (a small house occupied by the Twilights when they first came to Brownington), and the Cyrus Eaton House, originally the home of a local businessman who sold property to the Twilights. It is now administrative headquarters of the society.

Old Stone House Museum contains 25 exhibit rooms with a variety of displays, all of which are related to Orleans County's history. Most of the exhibits relate to specific themes such as lighting devices, toys, farm tools or quilts and coverlets, and some rooms, such as the original kitchen and a bedroom, are furnished as period rooms.

The large New England farmhouse that Twilight built for his family—and to accommodate several boarding students—still stands on nearby property (privately owned). The original Orleans County Grammar School Building, now used as a Grange Hall, is located nearby, as is the Brownington Congregational Church where Twilight preached. The museum is open every day during July and August and on spring and fall weekends. Call 802-754-2022 for information.

$3.50 (for French lessons). Twilight was considered a stern disiplinarian but had a kind, fatherly appeal as well. There were more than 100 students at the school during the next decade, and at least one-third of them were young women.

In 1847 another dispute erupted between Twilight and the school trustees. Twilight sold the dormitory to them and he and his wife left Brownington for Canada. Without his direction, however, the school floundered miserably and within a few years, the trustees were forced to ask Twilight to return to the academy. He and his wife returned with great fanfare; unfortunately, two years later he suffered a stroke and died in 1857. Within another two years, the academy, which could not survive without him, closed its doors forever.

After many years of being abandoned, the building was rescued by the Orleans County Historical Society. Today it serves as a museum filled with exhibits of local interest. Some objects are directly associated with the Twilights and the original, groundbreaking school.

Route 123
Mason, N.H.
207-878-2070

OPEN:
Weekdays: 11–3

ADMISSION:
Free

The Mann House

Mason, New Hampshire
1 7 8 0

The house where Uncle Sam was born in Menotomy (now Arlington), Massachusetts, no longer stands, but a monument in the center of that town proudly marks the site. Many miles farther north, however, just over the New Hampshire border in the tiny town of Mason, another large marker stands beside a small red house proclaiming it to be the boyhood home of Uncle Sam.

For those who thought the national symbol of the United States—a tall, lanky white-haired man dressed in red and white striped pants, a blue jacket and a tall red, white and blue silk hat—was just a fictitious figure, these historical markers are meant to prove otherwise.

Samuel Wilson, alias Uncle Sam, was the middle child in a large family of 11 children. In 1780, when he was 14 years old, he and his family made the long trek from Menotomy, Massachusetts, to Mason, New Hampshire. It was a distance of less than 100 miles, but the roads were rough and the Wilsons had only two lumbering oxen to pull their overloaded cart full of belongings.

Sam's father, Edward Wilson, had invested his life savings in these two weary oxen and a plot of land in Mason where he and his sons would build a house and farm the land. Both he and his eldest son, Joseph, had served in the Continental Army, but Edward was now 48 years old and he turned to farming to provide a better life for his large family.

Once the house was built, however, Joseph and the next two oldest sons enlisted in the army, which left Sam as his father's right-hand man on the farm. It was a job he was good at, and the farm prospered.

Sam had time to attend school, learning reading,

writing and ciphering, which enabled him to keep books and handle business affairs. He also learned brickmaking from his grandfather (a brickmaker who had helped to build Harvard College) and his uncles back in Medford.

When Sam's brother Eben returned from the West Point Campaign, he told Sam stories about the fertile land along the Hudson River with rich soil and fine clay for brickmaking. The two brothers made plans to return to the area to go into business there. The place they chose was to become known as the town of Troy; Sam and Eben were among its earliest settlers.

They set up a brickmaking shop and, within a year, E. & S. Wilson was supplying quality bricks for many homes and public buildings in Troy, including the first courthouse of Rensselaer County. The brothers became well known and esteemed for their hard work and soon earned the nicknames Uncle Eben and Uncle Sam—"uncle" being a term of endearment at that time.

As business prospered, the brothers bought land and started their own farm. They raised cattle and swine and soon found themselves in the meat-pack-

The childhood home of Samuel Wilson, also known as "Uncle Sam."

ing business. They had their own dock where they could load their barrels packed with beef and pork and ship them on their own sloops down the Hudson River.

When the War of 1812 broke out, E. & S. Wilson was granted a contract to supply the army with beef. Also, Sam was appointed government inspector of meat. As the barrels of beef and pork arrived at the dock for shipping, those marked for the army were branded with the initials of the United States—U.S.— in 6-inch-high letters.

On one occasion, passengers were disembarking from a boat close by the Wilsons' dock and saw all the barrels with the large initials emblazoned on them. Curious, they asked what the "U.S." stood for. A guard on duty quickly answered "Why, those are Uncle Sam's initials!" Everyone within earshot chuckled, but from that day on the names Uncle Sam and the United States became synonymous.

Political cartoonists soon picked up on it, depicting the tall, gangly figure of a man dressed in red, white and blue as Uncle Sam—the symbol for the United States. Posters with the figure began to appear, stage characters started to impersonate him and, eventually, no Fourth of July parade was complete without being led by a colorful Uncle Sam. Uncle Sam Wilson himself took it all in good spirits. He was constantly being asked to be honorary chairman of committees and events, to give speeches or to make toasts. And when distinguished guests arrived in Troy, he would always be on hand to greet them and welcome them to the city.

Sam's mother and father had joined their sons in Troy but, when Edward Wilson, Sr., died in 1816, Sam's mother Lucy returned to her little house in Mason and lived there for the rest of her life. She died in Mason at the age of 98; Sam died in Troy in 1854 at the age of 88.

The small, red, clapboard cape-style house with a large center chimney in Mason is now privately owned, but can easily be viewed from the street. In the center of the village, however, is the historical Mann House (originally Captain Mann's Tavern) where Sam's wife, Betsy, lived. It is open to the public on weekdays by appointment only. The first floor is used mainly for town offices, and the second floor is headquarters for the Mason Historical Society, where research material and artifacts relating to the Wilson family are kept. For more information, call 603-878-2626.

Shop 'Til You Drop

Antiquing—along with house touring—is one of New England's major attractions for both visitors and residents. And collectors who flock to this part of the country throughout the year all have their favorite locations to which they return again and again.

One such area is along Route 119 (one of New England's scenic highways) which crosses the border of Massachusetts into New Hampshire just south of Uncle Sam's House in Mason. Driving south from Mason (Route 123 to Route 119), you enter West Townsend (Mass.), which is a good place to start hunting for fine antiques.

There are two locations in the center of town where large groups of dealers have combined forces to display an excellent selection of quality antiques: Antique Associates at West Townsend, 473 Main Street (508-597-8084), has 80 dealers, and West Townsend Antiques, 519 Main Street (508-597-8340), has 150 dealers. Both of these businesses are open daily, 10–5. There are several other shops in the same area. Most notable among them is Delaney Antique Clocks, 435 Main Street (508-597-2231), which has the largest selection of antique American tall clocks in the country. It is open on weekends by appointment, or by chance during the week.

Continuing farther south on Route 119, you will come into the center of Groton (home to the prestigious Groton School), where several more fine antique shops are located. Joseph Kilbridge Antiques, 134 Main Street (508-448-3330), is considered one of the finest and largest dealers in Massachusetts. It is open daily, 10–5. Pam Boynton, 82 Pleasant Street (508-448-5031), specializes in eighteenth- and nineteenth-century furniture and accessories. It is open by appointment (and sometimes by chance) on weekdays.

The dining room at the Old Tavern at Grafton is filled with nineteenth-century charm.

Yankee Hospitality

Old inns and taverns, often called "ordinaries," were an important and necessary part of daily life in Colonial New England. The term ordinary is derived from the British, meaning a place where all guests were served ordinary fare—a standard meal at a fixed price.

As early as 1634, towns were beginning to issue licenses to innkeepers. It was actually mandatory in those times for each town to provide accommodations for travelers and their livestock, and there were strict laws governing them. Regulating the consumption and sale of spirits was one of the main concerns of town officials. One old tavern sign, for instance, spelled out such restrictions, saying "a cupp each man at dynner & supp & no more."

With the advent of the stagecoach, more and more inns and taverns began to spring up along the "post" roads that linked New England towns and cities. Not only were the taverns and ordinaries a haven for weary travelers, they were the social and political gathering places for the local population as well.

Throughout the events leading up to the Revolutionary War, town taverns often became hotbeds of clandestine activities. They were frequently the rallying ground for the local militia.

There are many more such taverns scattered throughout New England, all of them with fascinating stories to tell.

Tales from the Wayside Inn

Boston Post Road
(Route 20)
Sudbury, Mass.
508-443-1776

OPEN:
Year-round
Lunch: 11:30–2:30
Dinner: 5–8

Longfellow's Wayside Inn

Sudbury, Massachusetts

1 6 8 3

Listen, my children, and you shall hear
Of the midnight ride of Paul Revere,
On the eighteenth of April, in Seventy-five;
Hardly a man is now alive
Who remembers that famous day and year.

When America was still dotted with one-room schoolhouses, nearly every school child memorized these five lines from Henry Wadsworth Longfellow's famous poem, *Tales of a Wayside Inn*.

On several occasions in the 1800s, Longfellow stopped at what was then called the Red Horse Tavern. The inn was almost 200 years old when Longfellow first saw it and he was intrigued with its antiquity and its history. Located midway between Boston and Worcester on the Boston Post Road in Sudbury, Massachusetts, it was one of the most popular stagecoach stops along the route. It was also, during Longfellow's time, a favorite summer vacationing spot for a group of professors from the Boston area—including many of his colleagues.

In 1683, John How (later spelled Howe) built the first inn on this site. Four succeeding generations of his family maintained inns here; the one that Longfellow came to know so well was built by How's son, David.

John's great-great-grandson, Lyman Howe, had become proprietor of the inn at the time of Longfellow's visits. He was most likely the inspiration for Longfellow's poem, *Tales of a Wayside Inn*. Lyman was a very hospitable host and, after dinner, the men would gather around the hearth in the parlor, where Lyman would regale his guests with stories of his grandfather's adventures during the Revolution.

In *Tales of a Wayside Inn*, Longfellow created a cast of characters based on real people he knew—a poet, a theologian, a Sicilian, a student, a musician, a Spanish Jew and the landlord. They, too, gather around the fireside at the inn, each one telling his own special tale. The most celebrated, of course, is that of the landlord. He, like Lyman Howe, tells the story of Paul Revere's ride. The popularity of this poem—and the association of Longfellow with the inn—prompted the name change from Howe's Red Horse Tavern to Longfellow's Wayside Inn.

Longfellow's Wayside Inn was renamed to honor the poet and his famous poem.

In 1923, Edward Rivers Lemon, owner of the inn, died. He left no heirs who could take over its operation. Henry Ford, the automobile magnate, was very interested in historical preservation. He purchased the inn and its surrounding 5,000 acres, bent on protecting and preserving its environment. He also arranged to move several other historic structures to the site, including the Redstone School (known for its famous student, Mary, and her little lamb), a working eighteenth-century gristmill and a general store. He later built the Martha-Mary Chapel on the property, a traditional New England-style chapel in honor of his and Mrs. Ford's mothers.

The inn suffered a devastating fire in December 1955. The building was almost completely gutted, and it was thought that the inn was doomed. But as news of the fire spread, contributions and offers began to flood in from across the nation, and the Massachusetts legislature passed a resolution calling for its restoration. Fortunately, about 80 percent of the original antiques survived the fire, including those in the parlor described by Longfellow in his famous poem.

The painstaking job of restoration was completed in 1958. Shortly thereafter, the Ford Foundation transferred its trusteeship to the National Trust for Historical Preservation. They, in turn, transmitted control to

Mary-Had-a-Little-Lamb School

Located on the grounds of The Wayside Inn is a restored one-room schoolhouse moved here from nearby Sterling, Massachusetts. This is the school where Mary Sawyer's pet lamb "followed her to school one day," creating for posterity one of the most favorite children's nursery rhymes.

The authorship of the rhyme has long been a controversial issue (Sarah Joseph Hale and John Roulstone seem to get equal credit for it), but the story of Mary and her lamb has been fully authenticated. The following incident was said to have occurred around 1815:

Mary Sawyer lived on a farm in Sterling. One morning when she and her father went to tend the animals in the barn, they discovered newly born twin lambs. One of them was sickly and the mother rejected it, so Mary took it into the house and nursed it back to health. It became her pet and followed her everywhere—even to school, as every child well knows.

The school remained in use until 1856 and was purchased in 1926 by Henry Ford and moved to its present location. It was in very poor condition and was completely restored, even using some of the original materials. The furnishings are authentic to the period and young visitors usually find a stop here a delightful experience. It is open during the summer months, and a schoolmistress or master is often in attendance. Call 508-443-2312 for information.

the local Trustees of the Wayside Inn Corporation.

The Wayside Inn continues to be the oldest operating inn in the country and, according to its sign, still offers "Food, Drink and Lodging for Man, Woman, and Beast." All ten guest rooms have private baths, are air-conditioned and are furnished with antiques. Horses are accommodated in the barn across from the inn. Breakfast is available for guests; lunch and dinner are open to the public.

The Old Tavern at Grafton

Grafton, Vermont

1 8 0 1

Intersection of
Routes 35 and 121
Grafton, Vermont
802-843-2231

OPEN:
May–March
Lunch: 12–2
Dinner: 6:30–9
Reservations
required.

Closed December
24–25.

The Old Tavern at Grafton has a long and proud history that goes back to the early stagecoach days. This inn was on the route used by commercial travelers from Boston to Montreal, and was frequently patronized by them. Although much restoration work has taken place here over the years, the building looks much as it did in its earlier days.

The tavern's most prosperous and interesting times began in 1865, when it was purchased for $1,700 by the Phelps brothers, Harlan and Francis. The tavern was in much need of repair and improvements; Harlan had just returned from the California gold rush with $4,500 in his pocket—a tidy sum in those days. It more than took care of the work that was needed on the tavern, and enlarged it considerably, as well.

The old tavern became a very popular spot with the Boston literary set during the mid-1800s. Rudyard Kipling, Ralph Waldo Emerson, Henry David Thoreau and Nathanial Hawthorne were among the visitors who stayed here. Many political figures and people in the entertainment business were also attracted to the tavern. Ulysses S. Grant came on December 19, 1867, during his first campaign for president. In fact, a copy of that page from the hotel register still hangs on the wall of the General Grant room in The Old Tavern. Two other presidents, Theodore Roosevelt and Woodrow Wilson, also stayed at the inn while visiting the area.

By the early 1900s, long after the Phelps brothers had died, the tavern went through a succession of owners and eventually fell into disrepair. Modern motels and hotels with private bathrooms and better heating and air-conditioning were in demand. The town of Grafton itself, with the loss of businesses and industry, had declined rapidly. By 1940, the town's population had fallen to an all-time low of 393.

Eventually people began to discover this peaceful little hilltown—the perfect retreat for summer vacationing. For at least three months each year, with the return of many summer visitors, the Old Tavern would do a brisk business once again. Then long-time vacationers began to buy up old farmhouses and renovate them for summer homes. As these vacationers reached retirement age, they opted for year-round residency, increasing the population of Grafton to almost 500 by 1960.

Even this was still not enough to keep the town's economy healthy. In the early 1960s, the only grocery store left in town closed its doors forever. The survival of Grafton was seriously threatened.

Luckily for Grafton, it had a fairy godmother standing in the wings. One of its summer residents was to help bring about the reclamation of the town and make it what it is today—one of the most charming, picture-postcard New England villages as well as a vital, self-sufficient town.

The Old Tavern at Grafton was a popular gathering spot for the nineteenth-century Boston literary set.

Mrs. E. Rodney Fiske of New York was a summer visitor to Grafton for many years, often contributing to local restoration projects. When she died in 1959, she left the bulk of her estate in trust to two of her nephews "to do something she would have liked doing herself."

It didn't take them long to decide to help save the lovely little village of Grafton. They used the money to establish The Windham Foundation, which set about purchasing and restoring important buildings in town. It also provided assistance for people establishing businesses, such as a grocery store and garage. One of their first projects was to rescue the floundering Old Tavern and restore it to its former

The Restoration of Grafton

Besides the Old Tavern at Grafton, the Windham Foundation has restored a number of houses and businesses in town, bringing a total revitalization to this beautiful little New England village. The breadth and scope of the foundation's endeavors is quite remarkable. In order to get a sense of what has taken place here over the past 30 years, a stroll through the town and a visit to the Red Barn behind the Windham Foundation Center on Townshend Road is the place to start. Here, old photos, memorabilia and the book *A Vermont Renaissance* chronicle the amazing story of the foundation and its effects on Grafton.

"Restoration Number One" is what the Grafton Village Store on Main Street is called. It was the first project of the Foundation in 1963. Since then, other businesses in town have received a real boost from the foundation—the Grafton Village Nursery, the Grafton Village Garage and the Grafton Village Cheese Company. Products from the latter are sold all over the United States, including Alaska and Hawaii. The cheese company is open to visitors. The Cricketers Gift Shop is also owned by the foundation and is one of the most popular gift shops in the area. A blacksmith shop, an art gallery, the Old Tavern Stables and the Grafton Historical Society are all housed in buildings restored by the foundation. It's a fascinating story to hear and see and a beautiful village to visit. Call 802-843-2211 for information.

glory. And they succeeded, evidenced by the fact that it is now considered one of the top ten inns in the United States. It prides itself on offering to its guests peace and quiet—two rare commodities in today's unsettled world.

The inn has 35 rooms in the main tavern building, as well as five guest houses (each sleeps seven to nine people; most have full kitchens). The dining room offers breakfast to guests; lunch and dinner are open to the public.

The White Horse Tavern

Newport, Rhode Island

1673

Intersection of
Marlborough &
Farewell Streets
Newport, R.I.
401-849-3600

OPEN:
Year-round
Daily: Lunch and
dinner
Sunday: Brunch
Closed Tuesday
lunch.
Reservations
required.

The White Horse Tavern in Newport, Rhode Island, is considered the oldest tavern structure in the country. It began as a typical two-room, two-story residence for the family of Francis Brinley sometime prior to 1673. Records show that it was purchased that year by William Mayes, father of the notorious pirate of the same name. He obtained a tavern license in 1687.

Legend has it that in 1702, the younger Mayes gave up his wicked ways at sea, returned to Newport to settle down and followed his father as innkeeper at the tavern. It is believed that he brought back most of the plunder he acquired from his encounters on the Red Sea and hid it in the tavern. Rather then being ostracized, although somewhat of an embarrassment to the British colonial officials, he was heartily welcomed back by the local citizens of Newport. His newly granted license permitted him to sell "all sorts of Strong Drink," which added to his popularity.

A few years later, Mayes' sister, Mary, and her husband, Robert Nichols, took over the operation of the tavern. It was to remain in the Nichols family for the next 200 years (with only one short interruption). The Nichols family gave it the name of the White Horse Tavern—the horse being a popular symbol for taverns in those days. (Since few people could read at that time, it was a great advantage to be able to give someone directions to a tavern that bore a sign of a red, black or white horse.)

The tavern had always been the center of local affairs in Newport. Prior to building the Colonial House in 1739, both the general assembly and the criminal court conducted sessions there. This was of particular significance, since both Newport and Providence vied for the distinction of being known as the

capital of the colony. Newport was a wealthier and more populated town, and most of the early governors lived there. It rotated with the city of Providence as the seat of the general assembly. The two cities remained dual capitals until 1900, when the State House was built in Providence.

Much of the tavern's seventeenth-century interior flavor is preserved today, particularly in the old section of the building. Its heavy timbered framing is exposed to reveal chamfered beams. The massive central chimney still serves several original fireplaces. The exterior of the building is more representative of a typical eighteenthth-century Colonial Newport building, with its clapboard walls, plain pedimented front door and gambrel roof.

While the White Horse Tavern no longer offers lodgings, it is still well known for its excellent meals, served either in the tap room or in one of the several dining rooms. At lunch on Wednesdays, diners are treated to the curator's hearthside lecture—a brief history of the inn and its place in Newport's past.

Historic Newport

The White Horse Tavern is located in the heart of the historic district of Newport. Here in the narrow, crowded streets surrounding Washington Square—flanked by the Colony House and the Brick Market—are a number of National Historic Landmarks. A walking tour is the best way to view this section of town and two houses of particular note that are open to the public—the Wanton-Lyman-Hazard House and the Hunter House.

The Wanton-Lyman-Hazard House, 17 Broadway, is the oldest house in Newport, built about the same time as the White Horse Tavern. Some similarities in the interior details of the buildings can easily be noted. It is furnished throughout with period pieces and the kitchen features an exhibition of eighteenth-century cookery. Call 401-846-0813 for information.

Hunter House, 54 Washington Street, is considered one of the ten best examples of residential Colonial architecture in America. The interior is elaborately paneled and furnished in the manner of the wealthy colonial governors and ambassadors who once lived here. Rare examples of Townsend and Goddard furniture, early Newport silver, fine china and paintings are on display here. For information call 401-847-1000.

Visitors interested in historic religious sites will want to make sure to see the Friends Meeting House, 21 Farewell Street, built in 1699. One of the first meeting houses in the country, it served over half the population of Newport through the early eighteenth century. It has been recently restored, and is open by appointment only. Call 401-846-0813 for information. The Touro Synagogue, 85 Touro Street, dates from 1763, and is the oldest Jewish house of worship in North America. Founded by Spanish-Portuguese Jews, the service still holds true to their traditions. Guided tours are offered; call 401-847-4794 for information.

The Gris

Griswold Inn

Essex, Connecticut
1776

36 Main Street
Essex, Conn.
203-767-1776

OPEN:
Year-round
Meals and lodging.
Closed Christmas.

The location of the Griswold Inn, just a stone's throw from the banks of the Connecticut River in Essex, Connecticut, has played an important part in history. The town of Essex has a proud past as a major ship-building center. The *Oliver Cromwell*, the first warship of the Continental Navy, was built and commissioned here in 1776, and Essex was home port to West Indies traders, privateers and coasting schooners through-out the age of sail. Not surprisingly, the walls in the inn are lined with an extravagant collection of marine paintings, considered to be one of the finest collec-tions of marine art in the country.

By the time the War of 1812 broke out, Essex was so well known by the British that marines sailed up the Connecticut River, burned all 28 ships in the harbor and seized the town. Although the shipyards were burned, the rest of the town was left virtually intact, including the Griswold Inn. The inn became British headquarters, but the tap room was open to the local townspeople. A tradition began then that survives to this day—a Sunday morning hunt breakfast. This elaborate, hearty buffet includes early American and British dishes such as kippered herring, creamed chipped beef and the inn's own patented 1776 sausage.

Affectionately called the "Gris," this tavern has never changed its name, nor has it lost its allure as the main gathering spot for locals and visitors alike. Built in 1776 by Sala Griswold, it was one of the first three-story structures in New England. When the original bar, located in what is now the lobby of the inn, proved to be inadequate, the innkeeper pur-chased one of the town's early schoolhouses and had it moved by a team of oxen to its present location be-

The Griswold Inn still offers meals and lodgings, as it has since 1776.

side the inn. This became the Tap Room, and it continues to be the liveliest spot in town.

Yachting has now replaced shipbuilding as Essex's prime attraction; all summer long the town bustles with sailing events and the Gris is bursting with seafaring types. All year 'round, in fact, visitors come to this small, peaceful river town just to stay at the Gris, enjoy its lively hospitality and explore the area's many historic haunts.

The inn remains active in local affairs. Its staff and innkeeper are involved in community activities and host special events for the town's many celebrations. There is a special table in the dining room set aside for the regulars. For guests, it offers 25 bedrooms, including suites—either petite or luxury—and such modern-day conveniences as air-conditioning and piped-in classical music. Continental breakfast is included and the "fine food and spirits" are served up in charming dining rooms named the Covered Bridge, the Steamboat and the Library.

Out to Sea

Just down the street from the Griswold Inn on the historic waterfront in Essex is the Connecticut River Museum. Housed in a vintage 1813 warehouse on Steamboat Dock, it seeks to preserve the history of the longest river in New England. First called by the people of the Algonquin nation "Quinnetukut," meaning "the long river whose waters are driven by wind and tide," it was of such importance to the early English settlers they simply called it "The Great River."

The museum exhibits ship models, tools used in navigating and shipbuilding and a collection of prints and paintings depicting early scenes on the river. Among the models is one of the *Oliver Cromwell*, Connecticut's first warship, built here in 1776. A full-size reproduction of David Bushnell's 1775 *American Turtle* shows in detail the first submarine ever constructed. Call 203-767-8269 for more information.

Riverboat cruises are available at Steamboat Dock as well as at nearby Deep River Landing. On the large *Becky Thatcher,* a multi-level riverboat that departs from Deep River, you can get an unobstructed view of both Gillette Castle (see page 15) and the Goodspeed Opera House (see page 17). Call 203-767-0103 for rates and departure times.

Maps and House Listings

Of the fifty houses described in this book, you are bound to find several that interest you. This section is designed to help you plan your house touring trips based on geographic location. Houses are listed state-by-state. Using the maps, you can plan a tour to include several locations in one day—or plan to drop in when you are in one of these towns. Be sure to call ahead and confirm opening hours.

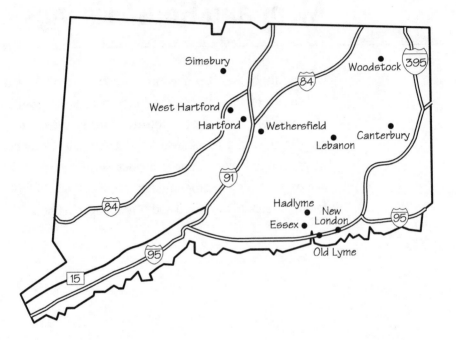

Simsbury

Woodstock

395

84

West Hartford

Hartford

Wethersfield

Canterbury

Lebanon

91

Hadlyme

New
London

Essex

95

Old Lyme

84

95

15

Connecticut

CANTERBURY
  Prudence Crandall House

ESSEX
  Griswold Inn

HADLYME
  Gillette Castle

HARTFORD
  Harriet Beecher Stowe House

  Mark Twain House

LEBANON
  Jonathan Trumbull House

NEW LONDON
  Monte Cristo Cottage

OLD LYME
  Florence Griswold Museum

SIMSBURY
  Heublein Tower

WEST HARTFORD
  Noah Webster House

WETHERSFIELD
  Webb-Deane-Stevens Museum

WOODSTOCK
  Roseland Cottage

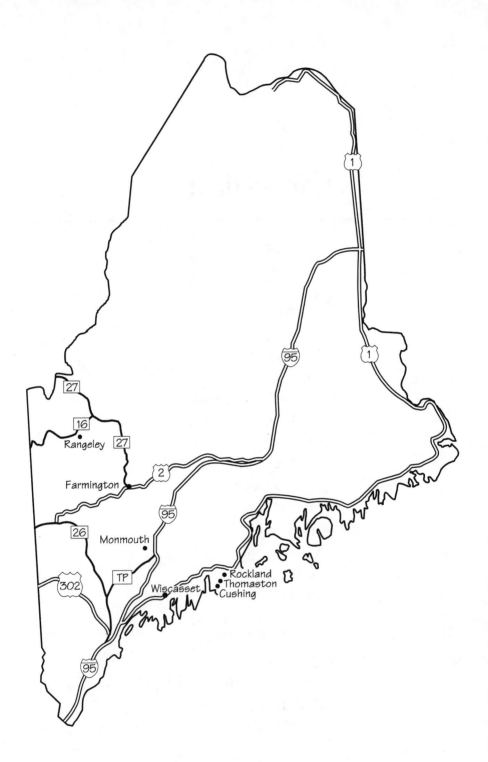

Maine

CUSHING
  Olson Homestead

FARMINGTON
  Nordica Homestead

MONMOUTH
  Blossom House

RANGELEY
  Orgonon

ROCKLAND
  Farnsworth Homestead

THOMASTON
  Montpelier

WISCASSET
  Musical Wonder House

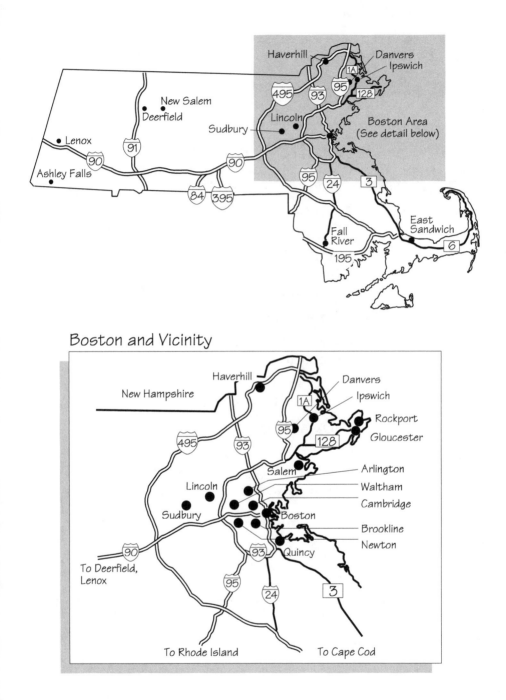

Boston and Vicinity

Massachusetts

ASHLEY FALLS
  Colonel John Ashley
  House

BOSTON
  Fenway Court

BROOKLINE
  John Fitzgerald
  Kennedy National
  Historic Site

  Longyear Historical
  Society and Museum

CAMBRIDGE
  Henry Wadsworth
  Longfellow House

DANVERS
  Rebecca Nurse House

DEERFIELD
  Old Indian House

EAST SANDWICH
  Green Briar Nature
  Center

FALL RIVER
  Brayton House

GLOUCESTER
  Hammond Castle
  Museum

HAVERHILL
  Duston House

IPSWICH
  The Great House

LENOX
  The Mount

LINCOLN
  Grange/Codman
  House

NEW SALEM
  Whitaker-Clary House

NEWTON
  Jackson Homestead

QUINCY
  Adams Birthplaces

ROCKPORT
  Paper House

SALEM
  House of the Seven
  Gables

SUDBURY
  Longfellow's Wayside
  Inn

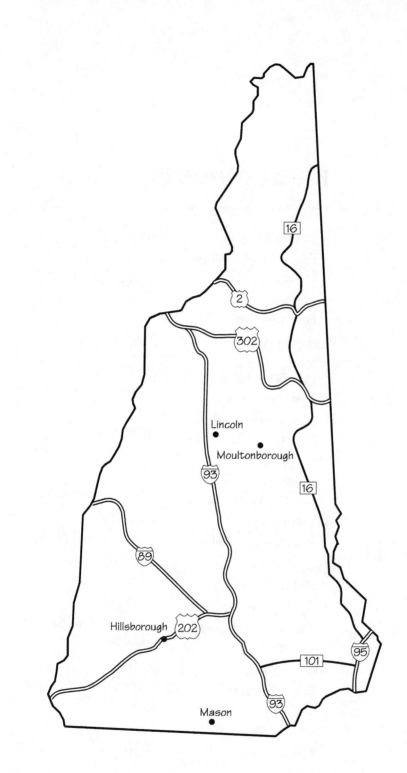

New Hampshire

Rhode Island

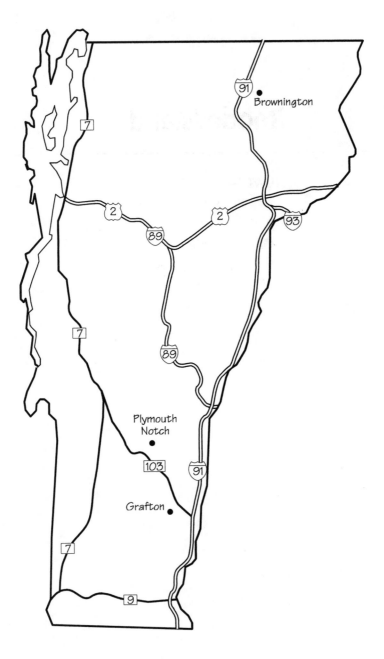

Vermont

BROWNINGTON
Old Stone House

GRAFTON
Old Tavern at Grafton

PLYMOUTH NOTCH
Calvin Coolidge Birthplace

Index

T

Tales of a Wayside Inn, inspiration for, 194–195
Tennis Hall of Fame, and museum, 20
Thornton Burgess Museum, 93
Trumbull, Jonathan, 174–175
Trustees of Reservations, The, 179
Twain, Mark, 41–44
Twilight, Alexander Lucius, 184–187

U

Uncle Sam. *See* Wilson, Samuel
Underground Railroad, 180–183

V

Vanderbilt, Cornelius II, 24–27
Vassall House, 53
Vermont, map of, 220

W

Wadsworth Atheneum, 47
Webb-Deane-Stevens Museum, 166
Webb, Joseph, house of, 166–168
Webster, Noah, 48–49
Wethersfield, Conn., historic district, 169
Wharton, Edith, 70–73
Whitaker-Clary House, 142
White Horse Tavern, 202
Whittier, John Greenleaf, 118
Wilson, Samuel, 188–191
Wyeth, Andrew, 85–87

Photo Credits

Hammond Castle Museum: Mary Maynard
Castle in the Clouds: Mary Maynard
Gillette Castle: Mary Maynard
Belcourt Castle: Beth Ludwig. Photo reprinted courtesy
of Belcourt Castle
The Breakers: Photo reprinted courtesy of The Preservation Society of Newport County
Longyear Historical Society and Museum: Mary
Maynard
The Great House: Mary Maynard
Montpelier: Mary Maynard
Mark Twain House: Photo reprinted courtesy of Mark
Twain Memorial
Harriet Beecher Stowe House: Photo reprinted courtesy
of Stowe-Day Foundation
Noah Webster House: Mary Maynard
Henry Wadsworth Longfellow House: Photo reprinted
courtesy of the Longfellow National Historical Site
House of the Seven Gables: Mary Maynard
Monte Cristo Cottage: Mary Maynard
Nordica Homestead: Photo reprinted courtesy of
Nordica Homestead Museum
Roseland Cottage: Mary Maynard
The Mount: Photo reprinted courtesy of Edith Wharton
Restoration, Inc.
Grange/Codman House: Mary Maynard
Florence Griswold Museum: Mary Maynard
Fenway Court: Photo reprinted courtesy of Isabella
Stewart Gardner Museum
Olson Homestead: Photo reprinted courtesy of
Farnsworth Art Museum
Green Briar Nature Center: Mary Maynard
Paper House: Photo reprinted courtesy of the Paper
House

Musical Wonder House: Photo reprinted courtesy of
The Musical Wonder House

Pickity Place: Mary Maynard

Heublein Tower: Photo reprinted courtesy of State of
Connecticut, DEP-State Parks Division

Russell-Colbath House: Mary Maynard

Blossom House: Photo reprinted courtesy of Monmouth
Museum

Dustin House: Mary Maynard

Farnsworth Homestead: Ben Magro. Photo reprinted
courtesy of Farnsworth Art Museum

Old Indian House: Photo reprinted courtesy of Memorial Hall Museum

Rebecca Nurse House: Mary Maynard

Fall River Museum: Photo reprinted courtesy of Fall
River Historical Society

Orgonon: Photo reprinted courtesy of Wilhelm Reich
Museum

Whitaker-Clary House: Mary Maynard

Adams Birthplaces: Photo reprinted courtesy of U.S.
Department of the Interior, National Park Service,
Adams National Historic Site

Franklin Pierce Homestead: Photo reprinted courtesy of
Hillsborough Historical Society

John F. Kennedy National Historic Site: National Park
Service. Photo reprinted courtesy of John F. Kennedy
National Historic Site

Calvin Coolidge Birthplace: Photo reprinted courtesy of
Vermont Division for Historic Preservation, President
Calvin Coolidge Birthplace

Webb-Deane-Stevens Museum: Mary Maynard

Prudence Crandall House: Photo reprinted courtesy
of the Prudence Crandall Museum Historical
Commission

Johnathan Trumbull House: Photo reprinted courtesy of
The Governor John Trumbull House

Colonel John Ashley House: Photo reprinted courtesy of
The Trustees of Reservations

Jackson Homestead: Mary Maynard

Old Stone House: Mary Maynard

Mann House: Mary Maynard

Longfellow's Wayside Inn: Mary Maynard

Old Tavern at Grafton: Photo reprinted courtesy of the
Old Tavern at Grafton

White Horse Tavern: Mary Maynard

Griswold Inn: Mary Maynard

ABOUT THE AUTHOR

Mary Maynard is a lifelong New Englander and full-time freelance writer. She has traveled extensively in the United States and abroad, including trips to Germany, Italy, Great Britain, China, Russia, Israel, the Caribbean and scores of U.S. islands.

Her articles on a variety of topics have appeared in *Ms.*, *Boston* Magazine, *Equal Times*, *Sojourner*, and many other periodicals. Her previous books include *Hassle-Free Boston*, a critically acclaimed guide for women, as well as other travel guides to New England—*Island Hopping in New England*, *Open Houses in New England*, and *Dead and Buried in New England*.

Mary lives with her husband, Jim, in Weston, Massachusetts, and has three grown daughters.